Fun Engineering Activities for Kids

60 Fun STEAM Projects to Design and Build (5-10 ages)

Mary Badillo

Copyright © 2020 - All rights reserved.

No part of this publication may be reproduced, stored in a retrieval system, or transmitted in any form or by any means, electronic, mechanical, photocopying, recording, scanning, or otherwise, except as permitted under Sections 107 or 108 of the 1976 United States Copyright Act, without the prior written permission of the Publisher. Requests to the Publisher for permission should be addressed to the Permissions Department, Rockridge Press, 6005 Shellmound Street, Suite 175, Emeryville, CA 94608.

Limit of Liability/Disclaimer of Warranty: The Publisher and the author make no representations or warranties with respect to the accuracy or completeness of the contents of this work and specifically disclaim all warranties, including without limitation warranties of fitness for a particular purpose. No warranty may be created or extended by sales or promotional materials. The advice and strategies contained herein may not be suitable for every situation. This work is sold with the understanding that the Publisher is not engaged in rendering medical, legal, or other professional advice or services. If professional assistance is required, the services of a competent professional person should be sought. Neither the Publisher nor the author shall be liable for damages arising herefrom. The fact that an individual, organization, or website is referred to in this work as a citation and/or potential source of further information does not mean that the author or the Publisher endorses the information the individual, organization, or website may provide or recommendations they/it may make. Further, readers should be aware that Internet websites listed in this work may have changed or disappeared between when this work was written and when it is read.

CONTENTS

Introduction 7

Part One THINK LIKE AN ENGINEER 11

Chapter One WHAT IS AN ENGINEER? 12

Chapter Two HOW TO USE THIS BOOK 17

Part Two THE PROJECTS 21

TOOTHPICK TOWER 23

STRAW ROCKET 25

WATER CLOCK 29

PAPER TOWER 31

CARDBOARD TUBE SUSPENSION BRIDGE 34

HOUSE OF CARDS 36

RUBBER BAND GUITAR 39

CLOTHES HANGER BALANCE SCALE 41

PAPER PLATE SUNDIAL 43

STICK AND MODELING CLAY CABIN 45

PAPER CODING TREASURE HUNT 47

SHOEBOX FOOSBALL 49

CD HOVERCRAFT 53

TINFOIL BARGE 55

RECYCLED BOTTLE CAR 57

FANTASTICAL FLYING DRAGON	61
CARDBOARD CASTLE DRAWBRIDGE	63
CRAFTY RUBBER BAND SHOOTER	65
PAPER CUP TELEPHONE	67
SOLAR WATER DISTILLER	69
PAPER CUP SKYSCRAPER	71
BALLOON-POWERED BOAT	73
WATER ROCKET BLASTOFF	76
MAKING MILK PLASTIC	79
PIZZA BOX SOLAR OVEN	82
MINI SPOON-AND-STICK CATAPULT	85
TOY PARACHUTE	89
MIGHTY WIND METER	92
WATERWHEEL	94
PAPER CLIP HELICOPTER	98
RUBBER BAND RACE CAR	101
MARBLE ROLLER COASTER	105
SCISSOR LIFT GRABBER	109
RUBBER BAND PADDLEBOAT	111
DIY ELECTROMAGNET	115
EGG DROP CHALLENGE	118
CARDBOARD TUBE MARBLE RUN	121

CRAFT STICK TRUSS BRIDGE 123

SHAKER INSTRUMENT 126

PIPE CLEANER MAZE 128

PENDULUM ART 130

PAPER BRIDGE PENNY HOLDER 133

MINI NATURE DAM 135

LEMON BATTERY 138

PULLEY BUCKET LIFT 142

TOY ZIP LINE 144

SCRIBBLE BOT 148

NEEDLE-AND-CORK COMPASS 150

POM-POM POPPER 153

CLOTHESPIN BALANCING STICK 155

GRAPHITE CIRCUIT DRAWING 158

SIMPLE SHELTER 160

Part Three PUTTING IT ALL TOGETHER **163**

I'M AN ENGINEER! 164

ENGINEERING ALL AROUND YOU 165

ENGINEERS RULE 166

GLOSSARY 167

RESOURCES 169

Introduction

Hello, and welcome to *Fun Engineering Activities for Kids*!

Do you know a child who is inquisitive and loves to build and explore? This book is perfect to help foster creativity and strengthen those natural engineering skills that all kids are born with. In this book, you will find 52 fun engineering projects for kids ages 5–10 that will challenge and delight them. Along the way, they will learn about engineering and its relationship to STEAM.

Ever since I was a little girl, I have loved teaching. (Just ask my younger brother, who had to sit through hours of playing school.) I studied to become a teacher, and earned my master's degree in education. I enjoy creating fun, hands-on learning activities and watching children's faces light up when they "get it." I am blessed to be able to do this every day with my own kids now that I am homeschooling.

I married into an engineering family. My husband is a computer engineer, and my father-in-law and brother-in-law are both engineers. My kids are surrounded by engineers, and we enjoy doing engineering activities together as a family. It's not unusual to find our kitchen table covered with the kids' latest projects. From designing and building wooden dollhouses with secret passageways to gathering together on the living room floor with colorful plastic blocks, there is always some form of engineering going on at our house.

If you have school-age children, you are probably familiar with the acronym *STEM* (science, technology, engineering, math). The push to include *art,* to represent the importance of creativity and design, has led to the new acronym in the education world: *STEAM* (science, technology, engineering, art, math).

Engineering projects rely heavily on the various STEAM components. Mechanical engineers use science and math skills when developing safety harnesses for roller coasters. Computer engineers use technology and math on a daily basis. When civil engineers design new bridges, they use physics and math, and they incorporate art to design a bridge that is both functional and visually appealing. To help kids see the connection between engineering and STEAM, there is a brief explanation of the different STEAM components used for each engineering project in this book.

The projects in this book are fun! Kids will have the chance to design and build a variety of engineering projects that will strengthen their creativity and encourage them to be thinkers.

Each project has clear step-by-step instructions. Some projects will require an adult's help, but many are ones that kids can accomplish on their own, which fosters independence and a sense of pride in their work.

Just as each project lists which STEAM components are involved, each also includes a section that explains the hows and whys behind it. This section is written in easy-to-understand language with children in mind. Kids can use what they learn from this section to design their own engineering projects in the future.

You likely already have many of the materials needed for these projects at home. Items you don't have will be inexpensive and easy to find. In fact, most materials can be found at a local dollar store.

You may want to gather the most frequently used items in this book and create your very own "maker space." A maker space is an area that facilitates creativity. Having all the materials easily accessible in one place eliminates the need to search the house for just the right item.

You can easily tailor your maker space to fit your needs and the space you have. It could be something as simple as a large plastic bin in which you store craft sticks, pipe cleaners, tape, empty cardboard tubes, and other materials. Or, if space permits, it could be a kitchen cabinet or a bookshelf with plastic shoeboxes to help organize craft supplies and other building materials.

Along with the awesome activities in this book, you will find sidebars that feature real engineers talking about their field. These offer kids a glimpse into the life of an engineer, the lessons they've learned, and some of their favorite projects.

Engineering skills aren't just important for kids who plan to become engineers. Being able to ask questions, imagine possible solutions, think creatively, and problem-solve are skills that will enable a child to be successful no matter what career they choose. And, don't forget, engineering projects are tons of fun, too!

Part One THINK LIKE AN ENGINEER

From designing marble roller coasters and building miniature bridges to testing out straw rockets, there are so many fun and exciting engineering projects for kids. But what makes an activity an engineering project and not just an ordinary kids' activity?

Engineering revolves around problem-solving. But what exactly do engineers do? Do they have a process they follow? What skills do engineers need? What skills are used when completing engineering projects? You'll find the answers to these questions and more in this part of the book.

Chapter One WHAT IS AN ENGINEER?

Building with blocks, creating blanket forts . . . engineering activities are super fun! But have you ever wondered what it really means to be an engineer?

This chapter will help you understand what engineering is and give you a glimpse into the four main types of engineering. You will also discover what engineers do and find out about the engineering design process.

Once you know a little more about what engineers do, you'll learn about the skills needed to be an engineer now and in the future.

WHAT IS ENGINEERING?

Engineering is the process of using science and math to create or improve something that helps people or the environment. People who work in the field of engineering are called engineers. Engineers improve people's lives by solving problems. They may develop technology that saves lives, find ways to make roads safer, or improve farming techniques to help produce more food.

There are many types of engineers in the world. Most of these fall into the four main types of engineering: mechanical, electrical, chemical, and civil. The types of engineering often overlap with one another.

MECHANICAL ENGINEERING

Mechanical engineers deal with how things are made. They work with heat, mechanical power, and machines. They study motion, energy, and force.

A mechanical engineer might design and build new cars, or they could create more efficient refrigerators. Mechanical engineers could also help develop surgical robots, elevators, and safety harnesses for roller coasters.

ELECTRICAL ENGINEERING

Electrical engineers deal with electricity and power supplies. They are involved in designing, creating, and testing electrical equipment. Some electrical engineers deal specifically with electronics and computer software.

An electrical engineer might design a remote control toy or an electric engine for a car. Electrical engineers could also design new computer programs or televisions with better picture quality.

CHEMICAL ENGINEERING

Chemical engineers deal with chemistry and life sciences. They work with producing, transforming, and transporting chemicals and other materials.

A chemical engineer may help develop a new medicine to fight cancer or find a better way to produce food. Chemical engineers could also find new ways to make plastic or develop more efficient fuel sources.

CIVIL ENGINEERING

Civil engineers deal with infrastructure. They work on designing and building roads, bridges, buildings, and even dams. A civil engineer makes sure buildings and bridges can withstand earthquakes and hurricanes.

A civil engineer may develop ways to protect people and the environment from the harmful effects of fire and smoke, or they may help design a new highway. A civil engineer might also work with architects to ensure a skyscraper can handle strong winds or a new bridge is able to handle the weight of all the cars that will travel on it.

WHAT DO ENGINEERS DO?

You have probably heard of the scientific method in school. Just as scientists follow the scientific method, engineers have a process they follow. It is called the *engineering design process*.

The engineering design process, sometimes referred to as EDP, is a series of steps engineers use as they work to solve problems. There are five main steps in the process.

- **Ask**
- **Imagine**
- **Plan**
- **Create**
- **Improve**

ASK

Engineers must ask a variety of questions about the problem they want to solve. First, they must determine what problem they are trying to solve. Then they need to consider how others have tried to solve the problem in the past. What worked? What didn't work? Engineers may need to do some research for this part.

Engineers also need to ask themselves if there are any special requirements they have to follow. For example, do they have to use certain building materials?

IMAGINE

In this step, engineers brainstorm solutions to the problem. This is where it really helps to have a creative mind. At this point, all ideas are written down.

Once brainstorming is finished, engineers can narrow the ideas down, examining the pros and cons of each. Engineers may need to do more research to choose the best idea.

PLAN

Once a possible solution has been selected, it is time for the planning stage. Often one of the first parts of this step is making a rough sketch of the solution on paper. Engineers will also produce diagrams and more detailed drawings later during this step that will help develop the prototype (an early model of a product).

Another part of the planning stage is making a list of all the materials needed. This includes identifying all the people needed to create the solution, as well as all the tasks that must take place. An engineer will also figure out the budget needed during this step.

CREATE

In this step, engineers build a model or prototype using the drawings and diagrams from the planning stage. This stage of the engineering design process also involves testing the prototype. Because the engineering design process is flexible, engineers can return to the planning step if necessary. Or changes could even be made while building the prototype.

IMPROVE

This is the step in which engineers look for ways to improve the design. In this stage, they will ask questions that will help them determine how to modify the prototype. What works? What doesn't? What parts could work better?

Engineers go back and forth between this stage and the creating stage as they test, debug (remove errors), and redesign over and over again.

It is important to remember that the engineering design process is a cycle. That means engineers don't have to follow all the steps in a specific order. In fact, they will often move back and forth between the steps. They may even choose to start over.

Notes from the Field

"I love being an engineer because I get to solve puzzles—I fix processes by investigating for clues, learning, and problem-solving. It's something new every day!

"My favorite project was developing a new assembly process. We had to automate an outdated process by combining different machines to work together. We wrote new programs, tried out new concepts, and failed until we succeeded! It was so rewarding to see the transformation that my hands helped build."

—Erin Gdaniec, manufacturing engineer, SSBB, Parker Hannifin Corporation

WHAT DO I NEED TO KNOW TO BE AN ENGINEER?

Do you like to build things with blocks? Do you play video games that allow you to create characters and different objects? When you do these things, you are using your creativity and imagination. Good engineers use these two skills every day. Curiosity is also important to have as an engineer. Curiosity drives engineers to explore and create new things. Engineers also need good problem-solving skills. They need to be able to work alone as well as with a team.

All of the elements of STEAM (science, technology, engineering, art, math) are also important when it comes to being an engineer.

Engineers apply science as they develop new ideas. For example, a chemical engineer needs to understand polymers to design a hairspray that can hold hair in place while still leaving it soft to the touch. A mechanical engineer uses knowledge of physics to design a new roller coaster that does three loops in a row.

Just as technology is used in your home every day, it is also used every day by engineers. During the planning stage of the engineering design process, technology can be used to create drawings and diagrams with computer-aided design software. Engineers use 3-D printers to make models and prototypes quickly. Civil engineers may use video cameras to monitor the traffic conditions before making changes to roadways.

Art is also very important when it comes to engineering. Artistic people tend to be very creative, and creativity is essential for good engineers. Civil engineers use art to create buildings and bridges that are pleasing to look at while also being able to withstand earthquakes. A mechanical engineer will use art to design a new car that catches our eye and is energy efficient too.

Engineers use math every day. Careful measuring must be done to make sure parts fit together correctly. A civil engineer will use math to calculate how fast the water is flowing before designing a new dam. A computer engineer needs math to help debug a computer program.

As you can see, engineers use many different skills, and each one is useful in other careers as well.

Chapter Two HOW TO USE THIS BOOK

Are you ready for some creative fun? From building your own solar oven and electromagnet to creating a hovercraft, the engineering activities in this book are the perfect mix of learning and fun.

As you go through the book, you will notice there are several parts to each project. You'll see an estimate of how much time it will take to complete the activity. You will also find a list of materials and step-by-step instructions. A brief introduction before each activity will help you understand what each project is about. You will also find a section explaining all the hows and whys behind the project and new ideas to try that will take the learning further.

All of the aspects of STEAM work together in the world of engineering. For each project, a section explains how the different components of STEAM interact. You'll find that some of the activities rely heavily on just two or three of the components, while others blend all aspects of STEAM.

GETTING READY

Start by flipping through the book to get a feel for the types of engineering activities you can find in part 2. Choose a few that interest you. There is no need to start at the very beginning. In fact, you are free to skip around however you choose!

Check the difficulty levels for the projects that interest you. You may want to start with a project that is marked easy before trying ones that are marked medium or challenging.

Each activity has a short introduction that explains what the project involves and what you will be learning. Reading the introductions may help you narrow down which activities you want to try first.

Once you've chosen a project, look it over with an adult before starting. Pay close attention to the length of time needed to complete the activity. Many of the projects can be completed in 15–20 minutes, but some will require more time. Be sure you have time to complete the project and do any cleanup that is needed afterward.

Some activities include a word of caution. They could be extra messy or require adult supervision. It is important to pay attention to these warnings.

You will find that many of the materials required are items you already have at home. You may want to make a list of items needed for several projects so they can be purchased ahead of time. Sometimes you will be able to use substitutes for listed materials, such as using a piece of plastic tubing in place of a drinking straw.

DOING THE PROJECT

So, you've picked out a project to try. Now what?

Read the introduction so you are familiar with what the activity involves.

Next, read the instructions carefully all the way through. Each project in the book has step-by-step instructions for you to follow. Try to follow them as carefully as possible.

Most of the projects will work the first time. Sometimes you will need to go back and make small changes in order to get it to work. That is what real engineers do. They are constantly testing designs and making changes to improve them.

What if you can't get a project to work the way you want it to? See if you can figure out what is causing the problem. Was something not measured carefully? Did you skip a step?

Remember, mistakes are just another way to learn. Chances are, even if you can't get the activity to work properly the way it is written, you can figure out how to solve the problem. And, most importantly, you should have fun trying!

Once you finish the activity, be sure to read the section that explains all the hows and whys behind what makes it work. This section is full of science concepts and other knowledge that you can use in future engineering activities of your own.

As you do the projects, you may find some words you aren't familiar with. There is a glossary at the back of the book to help you with new science and engineering terms that are important for future engineers to know.

You can put all that new knowledge to use by trying the extra activities that are listed at the end of each project. These are ways you can have fun while taking the learning even further. Or, better yet, come up with your own ideas of how you can change the project. That's being an engineer!

All of the elements of STEAM are closely connected. Although the projects in this book are all engineering projects, you will also be using the other STEAM elements. Each project lists the elements being used so you can easily identify how they are connected.

Are you ready to get started? Now that you've read how to use this book and you know how the projects are set up, it's time to flip to part 2 and pick a project to try!

Part Two THE PROJECTS

Are you ready for some fun with engineering?

This section will give you a chance to design, build, and test a variety of projects. You will get to build a waterwheel and rubber band race cars, design a roller coaster, and even make your own plastic! Doing the activities will teach you much more than just engineering. You'll be learning to ask questions, think creatively, and problem-solve, all while having fun.

Let's get started!

TOOTHPICK TOWER

When the Eiffel Tower was built in the 1880s, it was the tallest human-made structure in the world. The design of the tower incorporated lots of triangles to help make it strong. In this challenge, you will learn how today's engineers use geometry to design and build cell phone towers and tall buildings.

TIME: 30 MINUTES

DIFFICULTY LEVEL: EASY

MATERIALS NEEDED:

- Box of rounded toothpicks (these are stronger than flat toothpicks)
- Mini marshmallows
- Tape measure

CAUTION: Remember, toothpicks are pointy! Be careful not to jab your finger and make sure all toothpicks are picked up after the activity.

THE STEPS:

1. Insert a toothpick into one mini marshmallow. Add another marshmallow to the toothpick's other end.
2. Continue connecting toothpicks and marshmallows. Can you build a triangle? How about a square?
3. Once you've made a few simple shapes, try to build a tower. How tall can you make it? Measure the height of your tower.
4. Once you've made one tower, see if you can make a taller tower. What helps make the tower strong enough to stay standing?

STEAM CONNECTION: **In this tasty civil engineering challenge, you are using the technology of a tape measure to see how tall your structure is. You are also using math (geometry) as you choose which shapes to use in building your structure. Finally, you are using art as you consider the appearance of your tower while you build.**

Hows & Whys: Just like a real tower, your structure needs a sturdy, wide base to prevent it from toppling over. You probably learned that the structure also needs to become narrower as you build upward. This keeps the center of gravity over the base.

What about the shapes you used? You may have discovered that triangles work the best to build a very tall structure. This is because triangles are very strong shapes. Unlike squares and rectangles, which are easily bent and deformed, triangles are able to hold their shape under pressure.

EXTENSIONS:

- Now that you've learned how to build a tall tower, can you use that knowledge to build a toothpick-and-marshmallow structure that is 6 inches tall and will support the weight of a small book?
- Try using pieces of dry spaghetti instead of toothpicks. Does that make it harder or easier to build a tall tower?

STRAW ROCKET

Rockets are so much fun to build and fly! Real rockets take off by burning fuel. The burning fuel produces gas, which escapes the end of the rocket with a lot of force and sends the rocket into the air. In this activity, you will build your very own mini rocket.

TIME: 20 MINUTES

DIFFICULTY LEVEL: EASY

MATERIALS NEEDED:

- Ruler
- 1 sheet of 11 x 8.5-inch paper
- Scissors
- Colored pencils or markers
- Clear tape
- Plastic drinking straw (or paper straw)
- Tape measure
- Scratch paper (optional)

THE STEPS:

1. Use your ruler to draw a rectangle that is 4 inches long and 6 inches wide on your paper. Use the scissors to cut it out.
2. Use the colored pencils or markers to decorate the rectangle with colorful lines or polka dots.
3. Flip your rectangle over, place a colored pencil or thin marker on one of the long ends, and roll the paper tightly around the pencil. Make sure the colored side of the rectangle is facing out.
4. Use clear tape to hold the paper so it stays rolled and remove the pencil.
5. Fold one end down ¼ of an inch and seal it closed with a piece of tape. You've made your rocket!
6. To fly your rocket, slide the paper tube rocket over one end of your straw. Hold the opposite end of the straw to your lips and blow. Liftoff!
7. Fly your rocket several times. Watch what happens to it while it flies. Does it spin in the air or does it fly straight?

8. Use your tape measure to see how far the rocket flies. If you want, you can record the distances on a piece of scratch paper.
9. Now make a new rocket, following steps 1–5. This time you will add 2 wings to the rocket. Draw 2 right triangles that are 2 inches tall and 1 inch wide and cut them out. Tape them along the bottom of the rocket on opposite sides.
10. Test out your new rocket. How does it compare with your first rocket? Does it spin or stay steady?
11. Use the tape measure to see how far this new rocket flies.

STEAM CONNECTION: **You are using all the elements of STEAM in this mechanical engineering activity. You are using science (physics) to help launch the rocket. Technology is being used when you involve scissors. Art is incorporated when you color the rocket and design the fins. You are also using math when you make the fins (geometry) and measure the distance of the rocket's flight.**

Hows & Whys: When you blow into the straw, the air travels up to the rocket. Once it hits the nose of the rocket, where you bent down the tube, the air is deflected back down the sides of the tube and out the bottom of the rocket. This causes the rocket to fly off the straw.

Adding fins to the rocket helps keep the rocket steady when it flies. The fins work just like the feathers on the end of an arrow.

EXTENSIONS:

- What happens if you add 2 more triangle wings to the rocket?
- How do different wing shapes affect the rocket? Try making rounded wings.

Notes from the Field

"I've lived in three different continents and worked on a variety of projects including flight-testing business jets, acoustic and vibration analysis of cars, systems engineering, and software design. The opportunities are endless."

—Sarah Deutsch, mechanical engineer

WATER CLOCK

Early watches only had an hour hand. Minute hands didn't appear on watches until the 17th century. Can you imagine that? Before modern clocks, water clocks were one way people kept track of the passing of time. In this challenge, you will learn how water clocks worked and how to engineer one.

TIME: 15 MINUTES

DIFFICULTY LEVEL: EASY

MATERIALS NEEDED:

- Thumbtack
- Plastic cup (must fit inside the jar's mouth without touching the bottom of the jar)
- Glass jar
- Pitcher of water
- Timer or stopwatch
- Permanent marker

CAUTION: Be careful when using thumbtacks. They can be quite sharp.

THE STEPS:

1. Use your thumbtack to make a small hole in the center of the bottom of your cup.
2. Sit the cup into the jar's opening, making sure it is snug.
3. Fill the cup with water from your pitcher and start your timer or stopwatch. The water should drip into the jar.
4. Watch your timer and when it hits 1 minute, use the permanent marker to make a mark on your jar at the height of the water level in the jar.
5. Make a second mark on the jar when it hits 2 minutes.
6. Continue watching the timer and making marks on the jar for minutes 3, 4, and 5.
7. Dump out all the water and start again. This time watch your timer and check to see how accurate your water clock is.

STEAM CONNECTION: In this mechanical engineering challenge, you are using the technology of a timer to create the water clock, which in itself is a form of

technology. You are also using math since you are dealing with the measurement of time.

Hows & Whys: Water clocks use the flow of water to measure time. For this clock you made markings for the passing time. When the water level reaches the first line, you know that one minute has passed. The same is true when the water level reaches the second and third line. Then you know it has been 2 and 3 minutes.

EXTENSION:

- Does the shape of your container influence how fast the water flows? Try using a recycled plastic bottle instead of the plastic cup.

PAPER TOWER

One of the things engineers must keep in mind when starting a new project is the limitations they may have. Usually there is a budget, meaning they have only a certain amount of money to spend. Sometimes they are limited by what materials they can use in the project.

In this challenge, you will build the tallest tower you can, but you will have limited supplies. It's a great way to learn how to think creatively and use your resources wisely.

TIME: 20 MINUTES

DIFFICULTY LEVEL: MEDIUM

MATERIALS NEEDED:

- 12 sheets of 11 x 8.5-inch paper
- 2 feet of masking tape

THE STEPS:

1. Roll one sheet of paper tightly along its longest side. Secure the center of the paper tube with a small piece of tape. Remember, you are limited to just 2 feet of tape, and you want to have enough tape to use when you start building!
2. Roll enough paper tubes to make a base for your tower. Connect them using a small amount of tape.
3. Once you have a base, it's time to start building upward. Use your imagination to build the tallest tower you can.

STEAM CONNECTION: **You are using science in this civil engineering challenge as you deal with the center of gravity for your tower. You are also using art as you design your tower. Finally, as you roll the tubes into cylinders and measure the height of the tower, you are using math skills.**

Hows & Whys: Rolling the paper into a tube helps you build a tall tower that can stay standing. That's because the rolled paper is a cylinder. Cylinders are one of the strongest geometric shapes because they spread force evenly throughout their entire shape.

EXTENSION:

- Try building a paper tower that can support the weight of a ball on top.

CARDBOARD TUBE SUSPENSION BRIDGE

Have you ever ridden in a car across a very long bridge? Most bridges that stretch a long distance are suspension bridges. In this engineering challenge, you will create your own bridge and learn how suspension bridges work.

TIME: 45 MINUTES

DIFFICULTY LEVEL: CHALLENGING

MATERIALS NEEDED:

- Hole punch
- 4 empty paper towel tubes
- Ruler
- Scissors
- Yarn or string
- Masking tape
- Cardboard
- 5 pipe cleaners

THE STEPS:

1. Using the hole punch, make 2 holes directly across from each other in one end of each paper towel tube.
2. Measure and cut 2 pieces of yarn that are 4 feet long each.
3. Tape one end of a piece of yarn to the floor.
4. Thread the free end of the yarn through the holes in 2 of the cardboard tubes.
5. Stand the 2 cardboard tubes up with the holes at the top so the first tube is 8 inches from where you taped the yarn. Secure this tube in place by taping it to the floor.
6. Measure 12 inches from where you placed the first cardboard tube and secure the second tube in place with tape, again with the holes up top. Make sure the yarn and tubes are in a straight line.
7. Stretch the remaining yarn and tape the end about 8 inches from the second tube.
8. Carefully pull the yarn between the 2 cardboard tubes down so it hangs down in a U shape. This will be one side of your bridge.
9. Repeat steps 3–8 to create the second side of your bridge. Secure this second side to the floor so there is 2½ inches between the 2 sides.

10. Cut a strip of cardboard that is 2½ inches wide and 28 inches long. This will be the road portion of your bridge.
11. In a real suspension bridge, cables support the bridge's deck where the road is. In your version, pipe cleaners will act as these cables. Bend one end of a pipe cleaner and hook it to the middle of the yarn hanging between one set of cardboard tubes. Stretch it across to the other side of yarn and bend the pipe cleaner to secure it in place.
12. Add 2 more pipe cleaners to the yarn in the same manner. These should be 2 inches away from the middle pipe cleaner on each side.
13. Set your cardboard road across the pipe cleaners. Adjust the pipe cleaners as needed so that the cardboard is level and the pipe cleaners support its bottom.
14. Add 2 more pipe cleaners, one on each side. Make sure the pipe cleaner runs under the road and is adjusted so that the road remains level.
15. To get your bridge's road to meet the ground on each side, bend the cardboard down on both sides of the road.

STEAM CONNECTION: **You are dealing with forces in this civil engineering challenge, which means you are using science. To build your bridge you used technology (scissors and hole punch). Art was involved as you designed the bridge. You also used math when you measured the yarn and the distance between your cardboard tubes.**

Hows & Whys: Suspension bridges suspend (or hang) the roadway by cables from towers. These towers support most of the weight of the bridge deck. The cables leading up to the towers and the cables leading to the ground also support weight and help transfer some of the force to the ground where the bridge is anchored.

EXTENSION:
- Test your bridge's strength by pushing down on the center of the bridge. Now un-tape the cables that run from your towers to the ground. How does this affect the stability and strength of your bridge?

HOUSE OF CARDS

Building a house of cards is a fun activity that has entertained people for decades. There are even competitions to see who can build the tallest structure. In this challenge, you will try building a card house. You will also learn about some of the different forces engineers deal with when building.

TIME: 20 MINUTES

DIFFICULTY LEVEL: MEDIUM

MATERIALS NEEDED:

- Deck of playing cards
- Tape measure (optional)

THE STEPS:

1. Balance 2 cards so they lean against each other at the top and form a triangle with each other and the table.
2. Do this again with 2 more cards, right next to your first set.
3. Carefully lay one card facedown across the tops of the other 2 triangles. (The point where they meet is called the vertex.)
4. Now try to balance 2 more cards against each other on top of this flat card.
5. Once you feel confident making triangles with the cards, try making a larger structure. How tall can you make it?

STEAM CONNECTION: **Because you are dealing with forces in this engineering activity, you are using science. Thinking creatively as you design your card house means you are also incorporating art into the challenge.**

Hows & Whys: In this challenge you are dealing with all kinds of forces. To get your cards to stand up in the triangular formation, you are balancing the force each card has against the other card. If the forces are unbalanced, one card will slide out of position and they will both fall due to the force of gravity. You are also dealing with the force of friction. Friction helps keep the cards in place.

EXTENSIONS:

- Try building a house of cards on carpet instead. How does the extra friction help?
- Try laying the cards on their sides and making squares instead of triangles to build a card house.

RUBBER BAND GUITAR

Acoustical engineers are a group of mechanical engineers who deal with vibration and sound. They may create better hearing protection for people who work in noisy environments, or they may design a better sound system to be used in a theater. In this activity, you will build a rubber band guitar to explore vibration and its connection to sound.

TIME: 20 MINUTES

DIFFICULTY LEVEL: EASY

MATERIALS NEEDED:

- Empty rectangular tissue box
- Empty paper towel tube
- Pen or pencil
- Scissors
- Hot glue gun
- 4 craft sticks
- Variety of rubber bands

CAUTION: Hot glue guns get very hot. A parent should assist you when using a hot glue gun.

THE STEPS:

1. Remove any plastic covering that may be on the hole of the tissue box.
2. Place the end of your paper towel tube in the center of one end of the tissue box. Trace around the paper towel tube.
3. Cut along the circle you traced to make a hole in the end of the box.
4. Push your paper towel tube about an inch into the hole you just cut out. Use hot glue to help hold the tube in place. This will be the guitar's neck.
5. Hot glue 2 craft sticks on top of each other. Then glue them to the box between the guitar's neck and the hole in the tissue box, perpendicular to the guitar neck. Glue them as close to the hole as you can.
6. Hot glue the other 2 craft sticks together, and then glue them directly below the hole so they are parallel to the other set of craft sticks you glued in place.

7. Stretch 2 to 3 rubber bands lengthwise around the tissue box on one side of the guitar's neck. It's okay if they don't all go over the hole in the tissue box, but the rubber bands should rest on both sets of craft sticks.
8. Stretch 2 to 3 more rubber bands the same way so they rest on the craft sticks on the other side of the guitar's neck. Try using rubber bands that are different thicknesses.
9. Try plucking the rubber band strings of your guitar. Notice how each rubber band sounds.
10. Now press down on one rubber band string where it hits the top craft stick before you pluck it. Does it change the sound?

STEAM CONNECTION: Since you are dealing with vibrations and sound waves, you are using science in this engineering activity. The scissors and rubber bands you use to build the guitar are forms of technology. You are also using art because you are building a musical instrument and music is a form of art.

Hows & Whys: When you pluck a rubber band you cause it to vibrate, which makes the molecules in the air next to it also vibrate. This vibration produces sound waves, which are what you hear.

Just like the strings on a real guitar, the thinner rubber bands make a sound with a higher pitch. This is because the thinner rubber bands vibrate more quickly than the thicker rubber bands do. Faster vibrations produce a higher pitch. The same is true when you press down on the rubber band before plucking it. This makes the section that is vibrating shorter and produces a higher pitch sound.

EXTENSIONS:

- What happens if you press down on one rubber band string where it hits the top craft stick AFTER you pluck it?
- Try making the hole in the tissue box a little bigger. Does this change the sound?

CLOTHES HANGER BALANCE SCALE

Have you ever played on a seesaw? When two people sit on opposite sides of the seesaw, the side with the heaviest person sinks to the ground. That's because a seesaw is a type of balance scale. In this activity, you will build your own balance scale and explore how it works.

TIME: 15 MINUTES

DIFFICULTY LEVEL: MEDIUM

MATERIALS NEEDED:

- Hole punch
- 2 paper or plastic cups
- Scissors
- Ruler
- String or yarn
- Clothes hanger with hooks or notches
- Drawer with a knob (to hang balance on)

THE STEPS:

1. To make the buckets for your scale, use the hole punch to make 2 holes in each cup. The holes should be close to the rim and opposite each other.
2. Cut 2 pieces of string that are each 1 foot long.
3. Tie the string to the cups so that one end of string goes through each hole, making a looped string handle on each cup.
4. Hang the clothes hanger over the knob of a drawer and pull the drawer out a bit.
5. Loop the string from each paper cup over the notches on the clothes hanger.
6. Check to make sure the cups are hanging at the same level and that the hanger is straight. Make adjustments as necessary.
7. Try out your balance scale by putting different items into the cups. You might try rocks, coins, or small toys. The cup with the heaviest items will sink the lowest and tip the scale.

STEAM CONNECTION: You used science in this mechanical engineering activity as you dealt with the forces of gravity. The balance that you built is a form of

technology. You also used math since you were dealing with weight and measurement.

Hows & Whys: Your scale is actually a type of lever, with the drawer knob acting as the fulcrum. The cup with the heaviest object inside is pulled down by gravity, tipping the scale. When the scale is in equilibrium, both cups hang evenly from the ground.

EXTENSIONS:

- Can you use your scale to find items that are different but are the same weight?
- What happens if you use a longer piece of string to hang one of the cups?

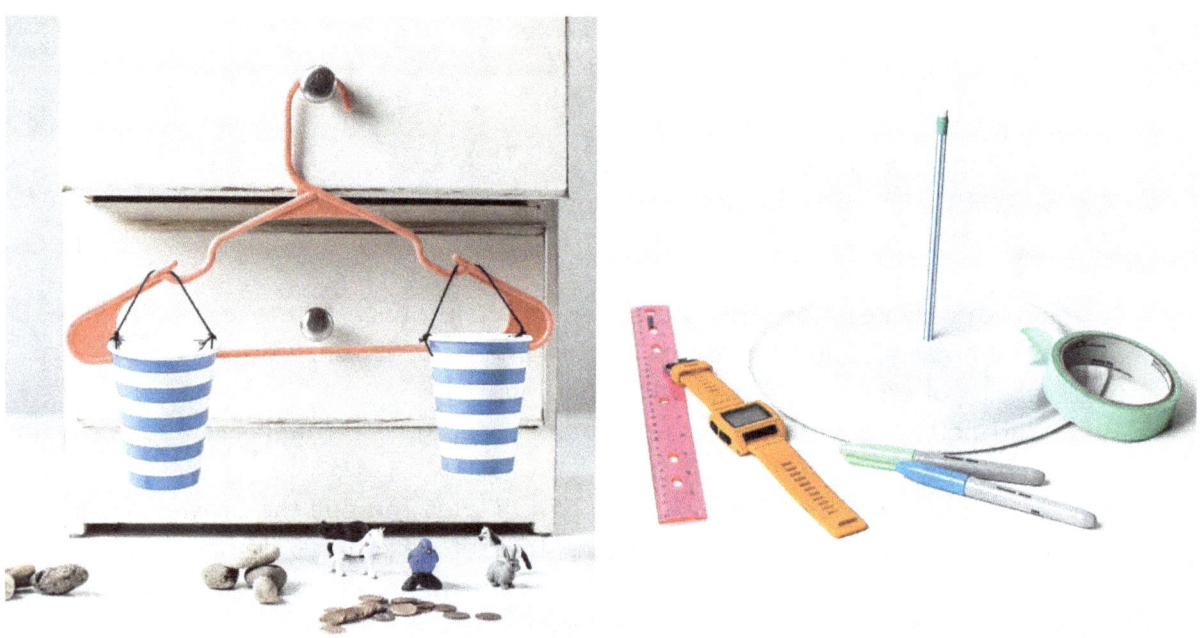

PAPER PLATE SUNDIAL

Before the invention of modern clocks and watches, people kept time by watching the sun and using the shadow on a sundial. In this activity, you will engineer your own sundial to see how you can use the sun to keep track of time.

TIME: 10 MINUTES TO MAKE, PLUS TIME TO MARK THE HOURS THROUGHOUT THE DAY

DIFFICULTY LEVEL: EASY

MATERIALS NEEDED:
- Sharpened pencil
- Thick paper plate
- Tape
- Permanent marker
- Watch
- Sunny day outside

THE STEPS:
1. Use the point of your pencil to poke a hole in the center of your paper plate.
2. Push your pencil through the hole, so the pointy end of the pencil sticks out from the bottom of the plate.
3. Place your plate in a flat area outside that gets plenty of sunshine. The plate should be upside down, with your pencil standing up. Use tape to secure your pencil if needed so it stays straight up. You may also want to tape the rim of the plate down so it won't blow away, or you can use a few small rocks to weigh it down.
4. Each hour on the hour, go outside and use your permanent marker to draw a line along the pencil's shadow on the plate. Check your watch and write the time next to the line you draw. Try to do several hours in a row if possible.
5. If weather permits, leave your sundial outside overnight and check its accuracy the next day.

STEAM CONNECTION: Since this activity uses the knowledge of how Earth spins on its axis and how that affects shadows, you used science in this mechanical

engineering activity. The sundial you created is a form of technology. And, since you are dealing with telling time, you also used math.

Hows & Whys: During the day, the sun seems to move across the sky because Earth is slowly spinning. The different position of the sun in the sky causes the shadow on the sundial to change. Each day the sun is close to the same position in the sky that it was the day before at that same time. This allows your sundial to be fairly accurate.

EXTENSIONS:

- Try making a more permanent sundial by sticking a strong stick into the ground and placing rocks around it to mark the hours. You can even write the hours on the rocks with permanent marker. It could be a fun addition to a flower garden.
- Stand in the driveway or on a sidewalk and have someone trace your shadow with sidewalk chalk. Mark the time next to your shadow. Go back and do this again, standing in the same spot. Check out how the shape and direction of your shadow changes in your human sundial.

STICK AND MODELING CLAY CABIN

Before modern building techniques, log cabins were often built as homes. Usually the homes started with one main room, and other rooms could be added on later. In this project, you will plan and engineer your own mini log cabin.

TIME: 30 MINUTES

DIFFICULTY LEVEL: EASY

MATERIALS NEEDED:

- Paper and pencil
- ots of thin, straight sticks
- Modeling clay or Play-Doh
- Old scissors (optional)

THE STEPS:

1. Use your paper and pencil to sketch out a plan for your stick cabin. Make sure you include a space for a doorway and at least one window. How many sticks high do you think it will be? Will you try to build a pointed roof or will you make the roof flat?
2. Start by breaking a couple sticks into 3- to 4-inch pieces. This is why you want very thin sticks!
3. Lay 3 sticks flat on the table to form part of a square. Where will your door be located? Break smaller pieces of stick for the fourth wall of your cabin, leaving a space where the door opening will be.
4. Roll thin ropes of modeling clay and use them to attach a second row of sticks on top of your first row.
5. Continue building your cabin, breaking smaller pieces of sticks as needed to form any window areas. A pair of old scissors may be helpful in cutting stick pieces all to the same length.
6. If you find that your original plan isn't going to work, you can change it! That's part of what engineers do; they create a project and make improvements as needed.

STEAM CONNECTION: You may have chosen to use the technology of scissors when doing this civil engineering project. You also used art as you drew your

plans and designed your structure. Since you had to measure the sticks against one another to make them close to the same size, you also used math.

Hows & Whys: In your version, the modeling clay helps to hold the sticks together. Log cabins that were built long ago had notches cut into their ends so the logs could fit snugly together at the corners. Pioneers would then seal the spaces between the logs with mud or clay, kind of like you are doing with the modeling clay. They called this daubing, and it helped keep out cold air.

EXTENSIONS:

- Try using a pair of old scissors to make small notches in the sticks and then using those notches to help hold your stick logs in place as you build your cabin. Does this help make your cabin more stable?
- Can you build a second level on your cabin?
- Replace the sticks with pretzel rods and the modeling clay with icing. Have a parent help you use a knife to cut the pretzels into the size you need for building an edible version of the stick cabin.

PAPER CODING TREASURE HUNT

Do you have a favorite video game? Lots of different people work together to create new video games. Software engineers (a type of electrical engineer) or other computer programmers must write the codes for the graphics and all the actions you can do in the game. In this activity, you will write a basic code, using logic similar to what software engineers use.

TIME: 15 MINUTES

DIFFICULTY LEVEL: MEDIUM

MATERIALS NEEDED:

- 16 blank note cards
- Notebook paper
- Pen or pencil

THE STEPS:

1. On one note card, draw a treasure chest or write the word *treasure*.
2. On a second note card, write the word *start*.
3. Now lay all the note cards, including the treasure and start cards, in a square, with 4 note cards going across and 4 going down. It doesn't matter where you place the treasure or start cards as long as they are not right next to each other.
4. Your goal is to write a very simple code to get your friend from the start card to the treasure card. On your notebook paper, write the word *start*. This is the first step of your code.
5. Look at where the start card is and determine what the second step should be. On the next line of your paper, draw an arrow to show your friend which way to go.
6. Continue using arrows to show which way to go to get to the treasure. You should draw one arrow per line on the notebook paper. Each arrow represents moving one note card. So, a ← means to move one note card to the left, and a ↑ means to move one note card up.
7. At the end of your code, write *stop*. This tells your friend they are finished.
8. When you are finished writing your code, flip the *treasure* card over so it is hidden.

9. Have a friend follow your code. Can they find the hidden treasure? If not, is there a problem with your code? Check it and rewrite it if needed.

STEAM CONNECTION: In this software engineering activity, you are using computer science skills. An actual software engineer would be using computer technology. You have used the technology of a pen or pencil when writing your code.

Hows & Whys: In this activity you wrote out a series of steps for your friend to follow. These steps were written in a specific sequence. Writing a sequence is one of the basic steps of computer programming. Your friend was acting as the computer as they followed your code.

EXTENSIONS:

- Try the activity with 25 cards instead of just 16. This will allow you to have more steps in your sequence.
- Mix up the cards and write a new code. This time instead of using an arrow for every separate step, try combining similar steps. This is called repetition. For example, instead of ➡ ➡ ➡ try writing ➡ (3) to mean your friend should go 3 note cards to the right.

SHOEBOX FOOSBALL

Have you ever played with a foosball table? Colorful figures are spun around as opponents play a miniature soccer game. While it is fun to play, there is also a lot you can learn about physics from the game. You will engineer your own mini foosball game in this challenge.

TIME: 45 MINUTES

DIFFICULTY LEVEL: CHALLENGING

MATERIALS NEEDED:

- Permanent markers
- 10 clothespins
- Shoebox
- Ruler
- Scissors
- Hole punch
- 4 wood skewers
- Marble
- Colorful tape (optional)

CAUTION: Wood skewers have sharp, pointy ends. You may want to have an adult snip the ends off for you.

CAUTION: Marbles are a choking hazard for young children. Make sure all marbles are safely put away after this activity.

THE STEPS:

1. Start by making your foosball characters. Choose 2 different colors of permanent markers. Make 5 clothespins one color and 5 clothespins the other color.
2. Remove the lid from the shoebox.
3. Use your ruler to draw a rectangle on each end of the shoebox, measuring 2 inches long and 1 inch tall. The rectangles should be centered along the bottom of the box's ends.

4. Cut out both rectangles you drew. These will be the goals for your foosball game.
5. Use your ruler to measure the length of your shoebox and determine where the middle is. Mark this on both sides of your shoebox.
6. On one side of your box, draw a line 1½ inches to the right of where you marked the middle, going from the top of the box to the bottom. Then draw a line 1½ inches to the left of the middle marker. Repeat this on the other side of the box.
7. Now measure 3 inches up from the bottom of the box along these 2 lines and punch a hole. Do this on both sides of the box.
8. Thread a wood skewer through each of the 2 sets of holes from one side of the box to the other side so the skewers hang across the box. The skewers should hang evenly and be parallel with each other.
9. Now measure 2 inches to the right of the right skewer and draw another line from the top of the box to the bottom. Do this on both sides of the box.
10. Measure 2 inches to the left of the left skewer and make another line from top to bottom. Do this on both sides of the box.
11. Once again, punch holes 3 inches up from the bottom of the box along these new lines. Thread the remaining 2 skewers through these holes. Make sure these new skewers hang straight and are parallel to the others.
12. Clip 3 clothespins to each of the inner skewers. Make sure you clip 3 of the same color to each. Place one clothespin in the center and space the other 2 evenly on both sides.
13. Clip the other 2 of each color onto the remaining skewers so all of the clothespins of one color hang on one side of the box and all the clothespins of the other color are on the other side of the box.
14. If desired, you can decorate the outside of the box with colorful tape. Be sure not to cover the holes!
15. To play, place the marble in the center of the box. Rotate the skewers back and forth to hit the marble with your clothespin foosball characters. Try to hit the marble into your opponent's goal.

STEAM CONNECTION: In this mechanical engineering project, you are using all the elements of STEAM. You use science as you deal with energy, levers, and the laws of motion. You are using the technology of clothespins (which are a type of lever themselves). Art is involved as you color the foosball characters.

And you are also using math when you measure and make sure the skewers are parallel to one another.

Hows & Whys: The clothespins in your foosball game are a type of lever. The wood skewers are acting as the fulcrums for the levers. When the clothespin hits the marble, it causes the marble to roll. This is an example of Newton's First Law of Motion (inertia), which says an object at rest will stay at rest unless acted upon by an outside force. Your game is also an example of potential and kinetic energy.

EXTENSIONS:

→ What happens if you substitute a pom-pom for the marble? Is it easier or harder to hit it into the goal?

→ Can you design something to catch the marble when it goes into the goal?

Notes from the Field

"As a research and development engineer, I come in to work every day and face a new challenge—sometimes it's something no one in the world has tried before. It's exciting, it's fun, and it's empowering."

—Maggie Connell, chemical engineer

CD HOVERCRAFT

A hovercraft is a unique vehicle. Unlike a car that uses wheels, or a boat that floats on water, hovercrafts actually float on a cushion of air. Not only that, but they are amphibious, meaning they can travel over both land and water. In this activity, you will create your own hovercraft using supplies you probably already have at home.

TIME: 10 MINUTES

DIFFICULTY LEVEL: EASY

MATERIALS NEEDED:

- Drinking spout from a reusable water bottle
- Unwanted CD
- Duct tape
- Scissors (optional)
- Balloon

CAUTION: Balloons can be choking hazards for small children. Make sure to dispose of used balloons properly when finished.

THE STEPS:

1. Place your drinking spout flat over the hole of your CD. (Check with your parents first to make sure you can use the CD!)
2. Cut or rip your duct tape into 2-inch-long strips.
3. Use the duct tape to attach the drinking spout to the CD. Make sure you completely seal around the spout with tape so no air will leak.
4. Blow up your balloon and pinch the neck to keep the air from escaping.
5. Keeping the balloon pinched, stretch the mouth of the balloon over the drinking spout. This step is easier if you have a friend help you.
6. Place your hovercraft on a hard, flat surface, such as a table or floor.
7. Make sure the drinking spout is open, and then let go of the balloon.
8. Your hovercraft should float just above the surface.

STEAM CONNECTION: You are using science in this mechanical engineering project. Newton's First Law of Motion says an object at rest will stay at rest

unless acted upon by an external force. In this case, the CD stays at rest until the force of the air escaping the balloon causes it to move. If you do the first extension activity and time how long your hovercraft floats, you'll be using math and the technology of a stopwatch.

Hows & Whys: As the air leaves the balloon, it gets trapped beneath the CD. The trapped air greatly reduces the friction between the table and the CD and the air current then causes the hovercraft to glide across the table's surface.

EXTENSIONS:

- Use a stopwatch to time how long your hovercraft operates. Compare that time with how long it stays up when you only blow the balloon up partway.
- Can you make a hovercraft using a paper plate instead of the CD?

TINFOIL BARGE

Boats were one of the first forms of transportation, other than walking. The ancient Egyptians built boats from papyrus plants along the Nile River. Other early boats were carved from tree trunks. No matter what material you use, or what type of boat you make, the science behind what makes a boat float is the same. This activity will allow you to explore why boats float.

TIME: 20 MINUTES

DIFFICULTY LEVEL: EASY

MATERIALS NEEDED:

- Large plastic container or bathtub
- Access to water
- Ruler
- Aluminum foil
- Pennies

CAUTION: Even a shallow amount of water is a drowning hazard for young children. Make sure all containers of water are properly emptied when you are finished with this activity.

THE STEPS:

1. Fill your plastic container or a bathtub with at least 4 inches of water.
2. Tear off a 6-inch square of foil and fold the edges up on all 4 sides.
3. Pinch the corners together to make a good seal to prevent water from leaking into your boat.
4. Place the boat in water to see if it stays floating.
5. If not, experiment with folding the foil in different ways, and even different shapes, until you have a boat that will stay afloat for at least 10 seconds.
6. Once you are successful, carefully place pennies, one by one, onto the boat.
7. Count how many pennies your boat will hold.

STEAM CONNECTION: In this simple mechanical engineering challenge, you are using science because you are dealing with displacement to make your boat float. As you measure the foil and count the pennies, you are using math skills. You are also using art when you shape and design your boat.

Hows & Whys: Boats are able to float because of displacement. That means an object will float as long as it weighs less than the amount of water it displaces. Because water is very heavy, boats with lots of air in them are less dense than the water and are able to float.

EXTENSIONS:

- How does the size of your boat affect the number of pennies it can hold? Experiment with different-size boats and keep track of how many pennies they each hold.
- Try making boats of various shapes by molding the foil around different bowls and other objects in your house. Do any shapes work better than others?

RECYCLED BOTTLE CAR

The first car was made in the mid-1880s. No one could have imagined back then how cars would eventually shape the world we live in. In this activity, you will explore the mechanics of how cars move.

TIME: 30 MINUTES

DIFFICULTY LEVEL: MEDIUM

MATERIALS NEEDED:

- Empty plastic bottle
- Scissors
- 2 (6-inch) dowel rods (or a 12-inch wooden skewer, cut in half)
- Sharp knife
- 4 plastic lids of the same size

CAUTION: An adult should use the sharp knife in this activity.

THE STEPS:

1. Disposable water bottles are very thin, and the easiest for cutting, but you can also use another type of bottle for this activity, like an empty shampoo bottle.
2. If there is a label on the bottle, remove it.
3. If you are using a water bottle, pinch the side of the bottle about 2 inches from the bottle's bottom and make a small slit with your scissors. Use this slit to insert the bottom tip of your scissors and cut a small, round hole just big enough for the dowel rod to fit through. If you are using a thicker bottle, have a parent cut the holes for you.
4. Insert one dowel rod into the hole to determine where the hole across from it needs to be. This will depend on the size of your plastic lid wheels. You want to make sure the dowel rod (the car's axle) is positioned low enough that the wheels will be able to touch the ground. Also, make sure your axle is straight before cutting the hole. Your car won't work well if the wheels are crooked.
5. Slide one dowel rod through the holes you have made for the back axle. Use the position of the dowel rod to help you determine the best location to make the holes for the front wheels and axle. The front wheels should be parallel with the

back. Make sure the holes are cut at the same height as those you cut for the back.
6. Put the second dowel rods through the holes.
7. Have an adult use the knife to cut a small X shape in the center of each of the 4 plastic lids.
8. Push one lid onto each end of your dowel rods.
9. Try pushing your car across the floor. If the car doesn't roll, try adjusting the height of your axles or using larger lids as wheels.

STEAM CONNECTION: In the process of engineering your bottle car, you are creating and using the technology of a simple machine: the axle and wheel. If you choose to decorate your car, you will be adding in an art component as well.

Hows & Whys: This mechanical engineering activity is making use of the simple machine combination: wheels and axles. When the axle spins, it causes the wheels attached to it to also turn, moving the car forward.

EXTENSIONS:

- Want to give your car a smoother ride? Cut drinking straws to slide through the holes in the bottle and then insert wooden skewers through the straws to act as the car's axle.
- Add a paper sail to the top of the car and see if you can get the car to move when you blow on the sail.

FANTASTICAL FLYING DRAGON

Everyone loves getting to play with new toys. With a bit of creativity and a few simple items, you can engineer your very own flying toy. Or you can make one for a younger sibling to help keep them entertained.

TIME: 20 MINUTES

DIFFICULTY LEVEL: EASY

MATERIALS NEEDED:

- Empty cardboard roll
- Construction paper
- Glue
- Markers
- Googly eyes (optional)
- Scissors
- Ruler
- Yarn
- Doorknob or hook

CAUTION: Long strings can be dangerous to small children. Make sure an adult is present if giving this toy to a younger sibling.

THE STEPS:

1. Cover the cardboard roll with construction paper.
2. Design wings and a tail for the dragon and glue them to the back of the roll.
3. Use markers to give the dragon a face. Googly eyes would also be fun to use if you have some available.
4. Let the glue dry before doing the next part.
5. Cut 4–5 feet of yarn and hang it over a doorknob or from a hook so an equal amount hangs on both sides.
6. Thread the loose ends of the yarn through the top of the cardboard tube dragon and out the bottom.
7. Hold the 2 ends of yarn, one in each of your hands, and pull your hands apart, separating the yarn.

8. As you move your hands apart, the dragon will fly to the top of the yarn. When you bring your hands back together, the dragon will slide back down.

STEAM CONNECTION: **In this mechanical engineering activity, you are using technology and math when you measure and cut your yarn. Art is also involved in this project as you design your very own dragon.**

Hows & Whys: Pulling the yarn pieces apart increases the tension in the yarn and changes the angle of the yarn to the tube. The yarn works like a lever and pushes the dragon up. When you release the tension and change the angle back, the tube is able to slide back down due to gravity.

EXTENSIONS:

- How can you make the dragon fly faster or slower?
- Take the yarn loop off the doorknob. Can you make the dragon fly back and forth between you and a friend?

CARDBOARD CASTLE DRAWBRIDGE

Many medieval castles used a pulley-and-counterweight system to allow one or two people to raise and lower the heavy wood drawbridge. In this activity, you will explore how a drawbridge works by creating your own from a cardboard box.

TIME: 20 MINUTES

DIFFICULTY LEVEL: EASY

MATERIALS NEEDED:

- Scissors
- Cardboard box
- Ruler
- Pen
- Yarn

THE STEPS:

1. Cut the flaps off the top of the box.
2. Use your ruler and a pen to draw a large rectangle on the front of the box. The rectangle should be centered with its bottom edge being the bottom of the box.
3. Cut along the sides and top of the rectangle, leaving the bottom portion attached to the box. This flap will become the drawbridge.
4. Carefully use the point of your scissors to make a small hole about ½ inch from the top on both sides of the drawbridge. (Ask a parent to help you!)
5. Cut 2 pieces of yarn, 2 feet long each.
6. Thread the yarn through the holes in the drawbridge and tie a knot at the end of each piece so the knots rest against the outside of the drawbridge door.
7. Lay the remaining length of the yarn over the top so it hangs down the back of the box.
8. Pull the 2 pieces of yarn to close the drawbridge. Release the yarn to open it. (Depending on how hard you pull to close it, you may need to push it open with your hand.)

STEAM CONNECTION: Along with using engineering in this project, you also use math when you measure the yarn and draw the rectangle for the door. The ruler

and scissors are forms of technology. You could also incorporate art if you choose to decorate the box.

Hows & Whys: The edge of the box where the yarn rubs is acting similar to a pulley for the yarn to slide along. A simple pulley like this can be used to change the direction of force. The downward force when you pull on the yarn causes the door to lift up from the ground and close.

EXTENSION:

- What happens if you thread the yarn through holes made lower in the drawbridge? Does it make it easier or harder to lift the drawbridge?

CRAFTY RUBBER BAND SHOOTER

Rubber bands were invented by Thomas Perry in 1845. Rubber band toys have been around for many years as well. In this project, you will engineer your own rubber band toy and explore potential and kinetic energy.

TIME: 10 MINUTES

DIFFICULTY LEVEL: EASY

MATERIALS NEEDED:

- Hot glue gun
- 2 jumbo (6-inch) craft sticks
- 2 regular-size craft sticks
- Clothespin
- Rubber bands

CAUTION: Hot glue guns get very hot. Always have a parent assist you when using a hot glue gun.

CAUTION: Do not aim rubber bands toward people or animals.

THE STEPS:

1. Hot glue your 2 jumbo craft sticks together, one on top of the other. This will be your handle.
2. Hot glue your 2 regular-size craft sticks together, one on top of the other.
3. Use the hot glue gun to attach one end of the regular-size craft sticks about 1 inch from the top of your handle so they are perpendicular to each other.
4. Next, glue the clothespin so the part that opens is even with the top of your handle.
5. Let it dry completely.
6. To load your rubber band, pinch open the clothespin, put one end of the rubber band inside, and then close the clothespin. Stretch the other end of the rubber band to the front of your shooter and loop it over end of the small craft sticks.
7. Aim at a safe target (like an empty soda pop can) and release the rubber band by pressing on the clothespin.

STEAM CONNECTION: **Science is being used in this mechanical engineering project because you are dealing with potential and kinetic energy. You used technology (glue gun) and basic math as well when you built the rubber band shooter.**

Hows & Whys: When you stretch the rubber band, you are giving it potential energy. When you release it, the potential energy is quickly converted into kinetic energy, and the rubber band flies forward.

EXTENSION:

- What happens if you glue the clothespin in a different location?

PAPER CUP TELEPHONE

Most people know that Alexander Graham Bell invented the first telephone in 1876. But long before that, in 1667, British physicist Robert Hooke created a device that could transmit sound through a wire. Although his device couldn't compete with Bell's more advanced design, the simplified version of it in this activity does provide a wonderful way to explore sound waves.

TIME: 10 MINUTES

DIFFICULTY LEVEL: EASY

MATERIALS NEEDED:

- Scissors
- Yarn or cord
- Tape measure or ruler
- Sharpened pencil
- 2 paper cups

THE STEPS:

1. Cut a piece of yarn to be 10 feet long.
2. Use the tip of your pencil to poke a small hole in the bottom of each of your 2 cups.
3. Thread the yarn through the hole of one cup. Tie a knot to hold it in place inside the cup.
4. Thread the other end of the yarn through the bottom of your second cup. Secure it with a knot on the inside, too.
5. Ready to test out your new phone? Give one cup to a friend and have them place the cup over their ear.
6. Step away from them as far as the yarn allows, keeping the yarn tight, and hold the other cup over your mouth. Now, whisper a message. Your friend will be able to hear it through their cup!

STEAM CONNECTION: In this engineering activity, you actually created your own technology that uses the science of sound waves. By measuring the yarn, you

also used basic math skills. Want to add in art? Decorate your phone with markers or stickers.

Hows & Whys: Sound waves can travel through air, solids, and liquids. When you speak into the cup, the vibrations from the sound waves travel through the yarn to the listener's cup. Then the vibrations are transmitted to the air in the cup, around the listener's ear, allowing the whisper to be heard. Solids actually carry sound waves better than air, so the whisper is heard much clearer than if you were to just whisper it into the air from the same distance.

EXTENSIONS:

- Will the cup phone work with an even longer string? Try cutting a piece of yarn that is 25 feet long and testing it. Can you get it to work with an even longer cord?
- Try substituting plastic cups or tin cans in place of the paper cups. Does one work better than the other?

SOLAR WATER DISTILLER

The sun is amazing. It gives us light and helps keep us warm. On a summer day, the sun's heat can melt a candy bar. In this project, you will make a solar still that will use the energy from the sun to help purify water so it is safe to drink.

TIME: 10 MINUTES TO SET UP; 3-4 HOURS WAITING TIME

DIFFICULTY LEVEL: MEDIUM

MATERIALS NEEDED:

- Water
- Shallow plastic bucket or bowl (taller than your glass jar)
- Tablespoon
- Salt
- Sunny day outside
- Clean glass jar
- Plastic wrap
- Rubber band
- Rock

CAUTION: Even a small amount of water can be a drowning hazard for small children. Make sure to empty the water from the bucket when finished.

THE STEPS:

1. Pour 2 inches of water into your plastic bucket or bowl.
2. Stir 2-3 tablespoons of salt into your water.
3. Place your bucket in a flat, sunny location where it won't be disturbed.
4. Carefully sit your clean glass jar in the center of your bucket. Don't get any salt water in your jar!
5. Cover the bucket with plastic wrap. To make sure the seal is good, use a rubber band to hold the plastic wrap tight against the bucket.
6. Finally, place a small rock on top of the plastic wrap, right over the jar.
7. Let your solar still sit undisturbed for several hours.
8. When you check, there should be a small amount of water in your glass jar. Try tasting it. It will be fresh, without any salty taste.

STEAM CONNECTION: In this chemical engineering project, you are using scientific knowledge about solar energy. The solar still you built is a form of technology. You also are using math as you measure ingredients.

Hows & Whys: The sun evaporates the water in the bucket. The plastic wrap keeps the evaporated water from escaping, and so water droplets form on the plastic wrap. The rock on top causes the droplets to run toward the center of the bucket, where they fall into the glass jar. The water in the jar has been purified and is no longer salty.

EXTENSION:

- Rinse all the materials and try it again. This time mix a little dirt into the water. Don't drink the water at the end! Just check it to see if the solar still removed the dirt.

PAPER CUP SKYSCRAPER

Have you ever seen a skyscraper and wondered how they were able to build something so tall? There is a lot of engineering at work when it comes to building tall structures. This activity will allow you to explore some of the science involved.

TIME: 30 MINUTES

DIFFICULTY LEVEL: EASY

MATERIALS NEEDED:

- Stopwatch or timer
- 50 paper cups
- Tape measure

THE STEPS:

1. Set your timer for 10 minutes.
2. Use the paper cups to build the tallest tower you can in 10 minutes. It's okay if you don't use all the cups.
3. When the time is up, measure how tall your tower is.
4. Now try to build a taller tower, using what you learned from your first building experience. This time don't set a timer.
5. When it is as tall as you think you can build it, stop and measure the height of your tower. Is it taller?

STEAM CONNECTION: **This civil engineering challenge uses all of the components of STEAM. Besides engineering, you are using science as you deal with gravity and balance the cups. You are also using math and technology when you set the timer and measure how tall your structure is. As you design your structure and consider its shape, you are also using art.**

Hows & Whys: In order to build a tall tower, you have to start with a wide base. That makes it easier to keep the center of gravity centered over the base, which keeps the structure from falling down. Also, the higher you build, the narrower your tower needs to get. That keeps most of the structure's weight low to the ground, which also keeps it from falling over.

EXTENSIONS:

- Try using a pack of note cards with the paper cups. Can you make the tower taller if you layer note cards between the cups?
- Challenge a friend to see who can make the tallest tower in just one minute.

BALLOON-POWERED BOAT

Colorful balloons can be used for more than just party decorations. You can turn a balloon into a fun toy by using an understanding of physics. Make two of these balloon boats and you can race against a friend.

TIME: 15 MINUTES

DIFFICULTY LEVEL: EASY

MATERIALS NEEDED:

- Scissors
- Disposable plastic food container
- Bendable plastic drinking straw
- Balloon
- Tape
- Permanent markers (optional)
- Colorful duct tape (optional)
- Bathtub or large plastic container with water

CAUTION: Even a small amount of water can be a drowning hazard for small children. Make sure to empty the water from the bathtub or container when finished.

CAUTION: Balloons can be choking hazards for small children. Make sure to dispose of used balloons properly when finished.

THE STEPS:

1. Cut a small hole in the side of your disposable plastic container. The hole needs to be centered at the bottom of the container's side. Try to make it close to the size of your drinking straw.
2. Thread your straw through the hole you made in the container. The short end where the straw bends should rest inside the container.
3. Stretch your balloon and blow it up a few times. This will make it easier to blow up once your boat is made.
4. Slide the neck of the balloon onto the short end of your straw. Wrap a piece of tape tightly around the balloon's neck to secure it to the straw.

5. This is a great time to decorate your boat if desired. Use permanent markers to decorate the boat's body, or use colorful duct tape.
6. Fill a bathtub or large plastic container with 6 inches of water.
7. Blow through the free end of the straw to fill your balloon with air.
8. Put your finger over the straw's opening to keep the air from escaping. Make sure the straw is bent down so the end of the straw will be just below the water's surface.
9. Set your boat in the water and let go of the straw. Your boat should move across the water.

STEAM CONNECTION: You are using science in this mechanical engineering project. The scissors used to cut the container are a form of technology. If you decorated your boat, you also incorporated art into the activity.

Hows & Whys: Making a balloon-powered boat is a great example of Newton's Third Law of Motion: for every action, there is an equal and opposite reaction. In this case, the action is the air rushing out from the straw and pushing against the water. The reaction is that the boat moves forward.

EXTENSIONS:

➡ What happens if you cut the length of the straw? Will it affect how fast the boat goes?

➡ How does the amount of air you put into the balloon affect the boat?

WATER ROCKET BLASTOFF

Have you ever mixed baking soda and vinegar together? The bubbling reaction between the two is fun to watch. You can use that reaction for more than just a fizzy science experiment. In this project, you will use it to move a water rocket forward.

TIME: 20 MINUTES

DIFFICULTY LEVEL: MEDIUM

MATERIALS NEEDED:

- Small sharp knife
- Empty disposable water bottle
- Bendable plastic drinking straw
- Pen
- Duct tape
- Scissors
- Craft foam
- Bathtub or large plastic container with water
- Measuring cup
- Vinegar
- Tablespoon
- Baking soda

CAUTION: Only adults should use the sharp knife.

CAUTION: Even a small amount of water can be a drowning hazard for small children. Make sure to empty the water from the bathtub or container when finished.

THE STEPS:

1. Have a parent use the tip of a sharp knife to cut a small X in the center of the water bottle's lid.
2. Thread the short end of your bendable straw through the lid so that the bending part will be inside the bottle. You may need to use the tip of a pen to open up the cut more.

3. You want the straw to fit snugly, without gaps that air will escape through. If there are any gaps, use a small amount of duct tape to cover them.
4. Cut 2 triangles out of craft foam. These will become the fins for your rocket. Use duct tape to secure them to the sides of the bottle.
5. Fill a bathtub (or large plastic container) with 4–6 inches of water.
6. Pour ¼ cup of vinegar into your bottle.
7. Now for the tricky part. Tilt the bottle so that the vinegar stays at the bottom, and you can put a tablespoon of baking soda in without it touching the vinegar. You may need to push the baking soda in with your finger.
8. Keeping the bottle tilted, screw the lid on. Make sure the lid is on tight so no air can escape.
9. Give the bottle a quick shake and then place it in the water so the end of the straw is just below the water's surface. Your bottle should move across the water.

STEAM CONNECTION: **In this chemical engineering challenge, you are using science (chemistry) to power the boat. You are also using simple technology and math when you measure with the tablespoon and measuring cup. Art also plays a role when you design the rocket's fins.**

Hows & Whys: Mixing the vinegar and baking soda together causes a chemical reaction. This reaction produces carbon dioxide, which is a gas. The gas has to escape the bottle, so it pushes through the only opening—the straw. The escaping gas pushes against the water, causing your boat to go forward.

EXTENSIONS:

- Try changing the amount of vinegar you use. Does it affect the boat?
- What if you change the amount of baking soda?

MAKING MILK PLASTIC

Every day you are surrounded by things that are made of plastic. But today's plastics are very different from earlier plastics. Plastics we're familiar with now weren't around until the 1940s. Before then, toys and other items were often made with milk plastic, also known as casein plastic. In this activity, you will have a chance to make your own milk plastic.

TIME: 20 MINUTES, PLUS 2 DAYS DRYING TIME

DIFFICULTY LEVEL: MEDIUM

MATERIALS NEEDED:

- Small pot
- Stove top
- Measuring cup
- Milk
- Teaspoon
- Vinegar
- Strainer
- Sunny day outside
- Paper towels
- Silicone molds or cookie cutters
- Sandpaper (optional)
- Acrylic paints (optional)
- Permanent markers (optional)
- Spray sealant (optional)

CAUTION: Adult supervision is needed when using the stove.

THE STEPS:

1. Put the small pot on the stove top. Measure 2 cups of milk and pour them into the pot. (Note: 1% or 2% milk works best.)
2. Warm the milk on medium-low heat, stirring constantly, until it is just starting to steam.
3. Remove the pot from the burner and stir in 8 teaspoons of vinegar.

4. You will see curds starting to form immediately. Continue stirring for a minute.
5. Pour the contents of the pot through your strainer, over a sink.
6. Use the back of your spoon and squish the material that is left in the strainer to remove excess moisture.
7. Pick up the material in your hands and form it into a ball.
8. Place the ball on a layer of paper towels and place a couple more towels on top. Flatten it to remove a little more moisture.
9. You can now use your fingers to pack the plastic into your silicone molds. Or use a rolling pin and then cut shapes with cookie cutters.
10. Let your shapes dry completely. This should take about 2 days. To make the drying time shorter, remove the shapes from any molds after one day.
11. Once they are dry, you may need to remove some excess bits of plastic from the edges. You can use your fingernails or a bit of sandpaper for this.
12. *Optional:* Once your plastic is dry, you can use acrylic paints to decorate them. You can also use permanent markers to add details to each piece. A spray sealant will give them a shiny look.

STEAM CONNECTION: **In this chemical engineering project, you are using science (chemistry). You are also using technology and math when you measure the ingredients. The element of art is also being used when you form the plastic into shapes and later decorate it.**

Hows & Whys: Milk contains a protein called casein. When the warm milk mixes with the vinegar (which is an acid), the casein molecules unfold and form long chains. This is called a polymer. The polymer can then be molded into shapes.

EXTENSIONS:

- Try replacing the vinegar with lemon juice. How does that affect the plastic?
- Want to give your plastic a touch of color without painting it? Add a few drops of food coloring to the milk when you begin.
- Instead of pressing your plastic into molds, try making beads with it by rolling pieces into balls and using a toothpick to make a hole through the bead. When they dry, you can use them to make a bracelet.

PIZZA BOX SOLAR OVEN

The sun does more than just give us light. It is full of energy! Solar power is power that is generated from sunlight. It can be used for heat energy or changed into electric energy. In this challenge, you will use the sun's power to cook food.

TIME: 20 MINUTES, PLUS COOKING TIME

DIFFICULTY LEVEL: MEDIUM

MATERIALS NEEDED:

- Clean, empty pizza box
- Ruler
- Pencil
- Scissors
- Aluminum foil
- Tape
- Black construction paper
- Your choice of ingredients to cook (see step 6)
- Plastic wrap
- Sunny day outside

THE STEPS:

1. With the pizza box closed, measure and draw lines 1½ inches from both sides of the box and from the front.
2. Cut along your lines, making a flap in the lid.
3. Open the flap and wrap it with aluminum foil, shiny-side out. You may need to use a bit of tape to keep the foil secure.
4. Tape a second piece of foil, with the shiny side facing up, to the bottom of the pizza box. The foil should cover the bottom of the box.
5. Cut a square of black construction paper that is 2 inches shorter on all sides than your pizza box. Roll a piece of tape so the sticky side is on the outside, and use it to secure your black construction paper to the center of your pizza box's bottom, on top of the foil.

6. What will you cook in your solar oven? You can use it to make s'mores. Just layer graham crackers, chocolate candy bar pieces, and marshmallows inside on your black paper. You could also put tortilla chips inside and sprinkle them with shredded cheese to make your own nachos.
7. Once you put your ingredients inside, cover the bottom portion of the pizza box with plastic wrap. Use tape to hold it in place.
8. Set your solar oven in the sun. Position it so that the sun reflects off the foil on the lid's flap. Use your pencil to hold the flap open. You can tape the pencil in position if needed.
9. Check your solar oven every 10 minutes. Remove your food when it is ready and enjoy!

STEAM CONNECTION: **This mechanical engineering activity deals with energy. That means it is using science (physics). You are also creating your own technology, as well as using the technology of a ruler and scissors. Math is also involved as you measure before cutting the pizza box.**

Hows & Whys: Sunlight is converted into heat energy in this activity. The aluminum foil reflects the sun's rays into the box. The plastic wrap traps the heat inside, similar to a greenhouse. The black paper absorbs the sunlight and works to heat the food you place on top of it.

EXTENSIONS:

- How would using construction paper of a different color affect your solar oven?
- Place a thermometer inside your solar oven and measure how hot it gets inside.
- Try using your solar oven to melt broken crayons.

MINI SPOON-AND-STICK CATAPULT

Catapults were used in times of war during the Middle Ages. Sometimes soldiers would aim the catapult to fling rocks or other objects directly at a castle wall, hoping to knock the wall down. Other times objects would be flung over the walls. In this challenge, you will have a chance to build your own mini catapult.

TIME: 20 MINUTES

DIFFICULTY LEVEL: MEDIUM

MATERIALS NEEDED:

- 7 craft sticks
- Mini rubber bands
- Plastic spoon
- Pom-poms or mini marshmallows

THE STEPS:

1. Stack 5 craft sticks on top of one another and secure both ends together with rubber bands.
2. Next, stack 2 more craft sticks together and secure one end of them with a rubber band.
3. Carefully open up the 2 craft sticks you've put together and slide the stack of 5 in between them.

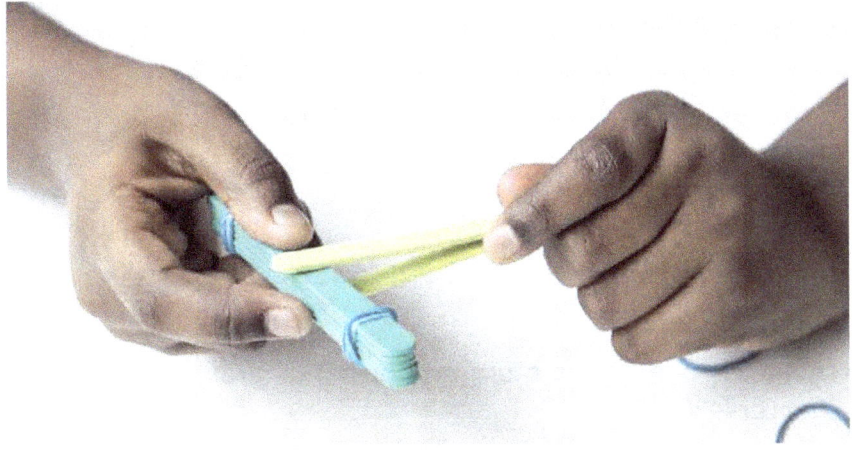

4. Secure your plastic spoon to the top craft stick using rubber bands. The bowl of the spoon should be at the top.

5. Finally, crisscross one or two more rubber bands around the area where the craft sticks all intersect.

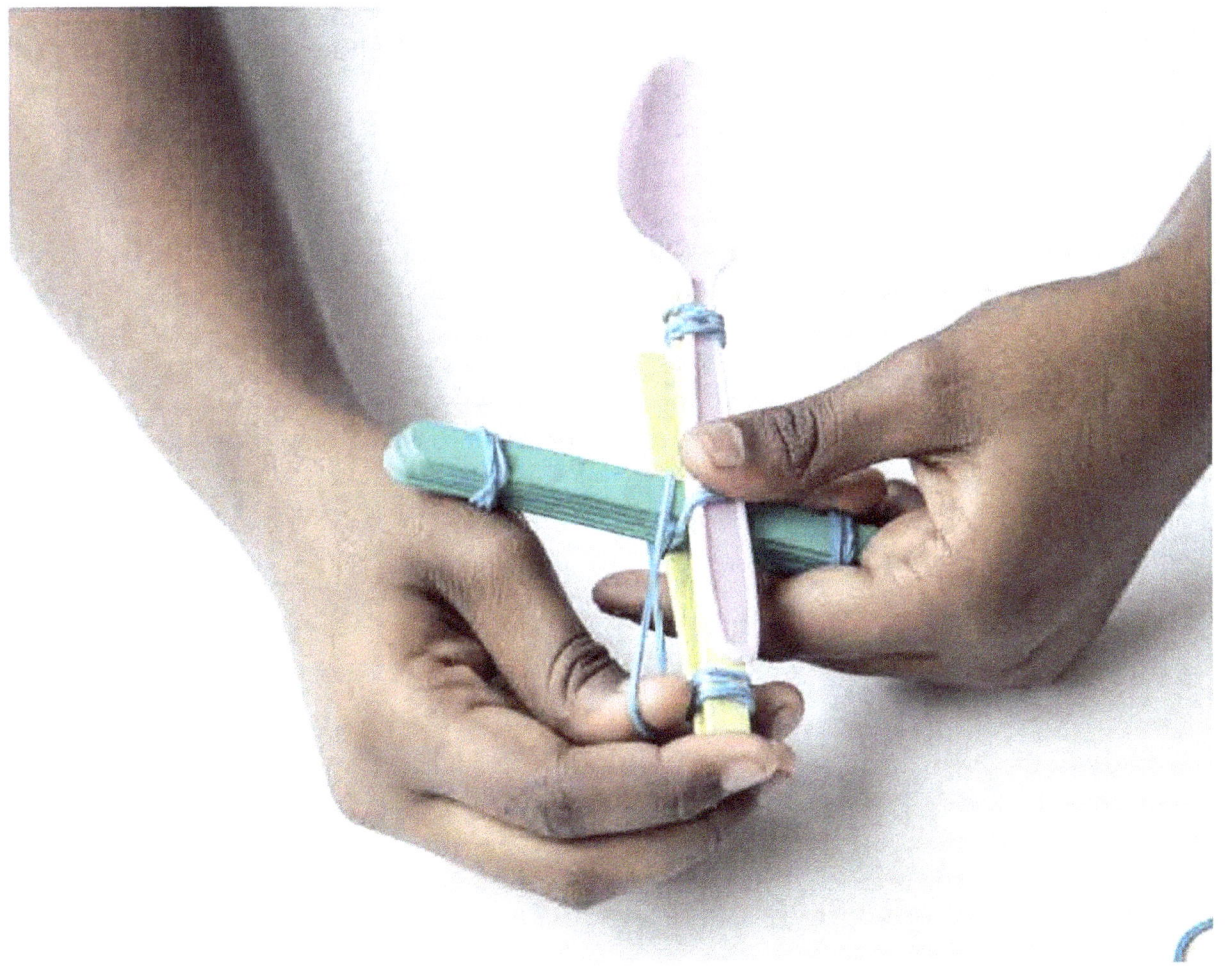

6. Place your catapult on a flat surface and use one hand to hold your crossbar (the 5 craft sticks) while pushing down on your spoon. Release the spoon to test your catapult.
7. If your catapult isn't springy enough, try adding another rubber band at the bottom or twisting the one that is there so it is tighter.
8. Once you are satisfied, try flinging pom-poms or mini marshmallows. How far do they go?

STEAM CONNECTION: In this mechanical engineering challenge, you are using the science of potential and kinetic energy. Because you are using this science knowledge to create a piece of machinery, you are creating technology. You are also using basic math skills as you count the craft sticks.

Hows & Whys: When you push down on the spoon, you are adding to the rubber band's potential energy. Letting go of the spoon allows the energy to turn into kinetic energy as the spoon pops back into position and the object you've placed on it flies into the air.

EXTENSIONS:

- Try using 3 craft sticks instead of 5 for the crossbar. How does it affect your catapult? What if you use 7?
- What happens if you move the position of the crossbar? How does it affect the catapult's performance?

TOY PARACHUTE

Have you ever watched a group of skydivers who have jumped from a plane? Their colorful parachutes are fun to watch as they float in the air on their way to the ground. This simple activity will allow you to explore how parachutes work.

TIME: 10 MINUTES

DIFFICULTY LEVEL: EASY

MATERIALS NEEDED:

- Chair
- Small toy figure (such as an army figure, toy block person, or plastic animal)
- Flat-bottomed coffee filter
- Crayons or markers
- Scissors
- String
- Tape (optional)

THE STEPS:

1. Stand on a chair and drop your toy figure. Notice how quickly it falls to the ground. What your toy needs is a parachute!
2. Open the coffee filter and decorate it with crayons or markers.
3. Fold the coffee filter in half with the colored side out and cut 2 tiny slits across the fold. They should be ¼ inch from the ends of the coffee filter.
4. Cut 2 pieces of string, 1 foot long each.
5. Tie one piece of string to the coffee filter through each hole.
6. Tie the opposite ends of the string to your small toy figure (or you can use tape).
7. Stand on a chair and hold your parachute as high as you can. Drop it and see what happens.
8. Does your parachute help slow your toy's fall?

STEAM CONNECTION: **In this simple mechanical engineering challenge, you are using science as you deal with the forces of gravity and drag. You are also using the technology of scissors. Art is also used when you decorate your parachute.**

Hows & Whys: The force of gravity pulls objects toward the ground. The parachute creates more air resistance than the toy has on its own. This air resistance (also called drag) helps to slow down your toy as it falls to the ground.

EXTENSIONS:

- What happens if you make the parachute smaller? Try using a cupcake liner or cutting a smaller circle out of a coffee filter to make a smaller parachute.
- What happens if you use longer strings? Try doubling the length of the strings you use and see what happens.

MIGHTY WIND METER

Have you ever been outside on a very windy day? The wind can be strong enough to blow a hat off your head or turn an umbrella inside out. The power of the wind can even be strong enough to turn large turbines to produce electricity! In this project, you will make an anemometer, or wind meter, to measure the wind's speed.

TIME: 20 MINUTES

DIFFICULTY LEVEL: MEDIUM

MATERIALS NEEDED:

- Scissors
- Corrugated cardboard
- Ruler
- Stapler
- 4 paper cups
- Colored tape
- Small recycled container with plastic lid
- Unsharpened pencil with eraser
- Thumbtack
- Timer

CAUTION: Be careful when using thumbtacks. They can be quite sharp.

THE STEPS:

1. Cut 2 strips of cardboard that are 1½ inches wide and 12 inches long.
2. Staple the strips of cardboard together to form a plus sign, but do not put a staple directly in the middle.
3. Decorate one paper cup with colored tape.
4. Staple the sides of the 4 cups to the ends of your cardboard cross, one cup on each end of the cross. Make sure all the cups face the same direction.
5. Set the cups and cardboard aside. Use the tip of your scissors to poke a hole in the center of the plastic lid of your container. (A small coffee can or icing container is perfect for this.)

6. Wiggle the scissors around in the hole to make it just slightly bigger than the width of your pencil.
7. Make sure the lid is on the container, and then slide your pencil into the hole, with the eraser end sticking up.
8. Use the thumbtack to fasten the cardboard and cups to your pencil's eraser. Make sure the thumbtack is as close to the center of the cardboard cross as possible!
9. Once your anemometer is built, you can take it outside to measure the wind speed.
10. Set the wind meter on a table. Set your timer for one minute and count how many times you see your decorated cup spin around. Engineers call this the revolutions per minute. Depending on how strong the wind is, you may need to hold the container with one hand. Or you could open the lid and put a few rocks into the container to weigh the container down.

STEAM CONNECTION: In this mechanical engineering challenge, you are using each of the **STEAM** components. Studying wind speed is something a scientist who studies weather (meteorologist) does. Not only are you using technology to make your wind meter, but the meter itself is a form of technology. Art is involved when you decorate the paper cup. You are using math when you count the times the cups go around and record your results.

Hows & Whys: When the wind pushes on the cups of the anemometer, they force the pencil to spin in the container. How fast the cups revolve can be measured in revolutions per minute (RPM). Faster wind speeds will result in higher RPMs.

EXTENSIONS:

- Use your wind meter to measure the wind speed every day for a week. Record the results.
- Set your wind meter several feet away from a fan and test how it reacts when the fan is set at a low speed and when the fan is set on high.

WATERWHEEL

Have you ever seen a waterwheel? Sometimes they are referred to as water mills. Long ago, waterwheels were used in mills to help grind flour and for other tasks. Waterwheels can also be used to generate electricity. In this activity, you will explore how waterwheels work.

TIME: 15 MINUTES

DIFFICULTY LEVEL: MEDIUM

MATERIALS NEEDED:

- Wood skewer
- 2 heavy-duty paper plates
- 6 mini plastic cups (3 oz. size)
- Duct tape

CAUTION: The point on a wood skewer can be very sharp.

THE STEPS:

1. Use the wood skewer to poke a hole through the center of both paper plates.
2. Flip one plate so the bottom faces up and arrange the plastic cups in a circle around the bottom of the plate. The tops of the cups should all touch the top edge of the plate. Try to keep the cups evenly spaced.
3. Secure each cup with a thin strip of duct tape.

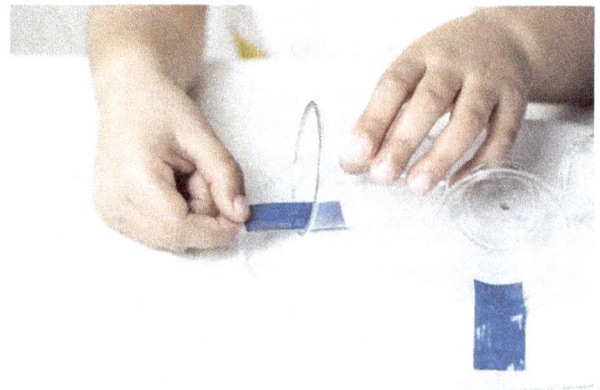

4. Thread the skewer through the hole in the paper plate.
5. Thread the other paper plate onto the skewer, next to the cups, so that both of the bottoms of the plates touch the cups.
6. Use small pieces of tape to secure the cups to your second plate.
7. Take your waterwheel to an empty bathtub or kitchen sink. Turn the water on so there's a gentle flow.
8. Hold on to both ends of the wood skewer and place your waterwheel under the faucet so that one of the cups fills with water. Watch what happens next!

STEAM CONNECTION: **When engineering a waterwheel, you are using science. The waterwheel itself is a form of technology. You are also using some basic math skills as you count the cups and place them evenly around the wheel.**

Hows & Whys: As the water fills the bucket at the top of the wheel, the weight of the water causes the wheel to rotate around the axis. Gravity causes the water in the bucket to spill below as the following cups fill. The cycle continues as long as there is water filling the top cup.

EXTENSIONS:

- What happens if you turn the water on faster?
- How could you change the waterwheel's design if you wanted it to work with water being directed at it sideways instead of having the water hit it from above?

Notes from the Field

"As an engineer, my favorite job so far was when I was on a team that put new computerized controls on a steam turbine that's large enough to power the city of Cincinnati. The computers on this turbine were out of date and beginning to break. The engineering team and I (very few engineers work alone) researched what new computers were needed, took measurements to be sure that the new computers would fit, and marked up large drawings to show the installers how to properly connect all the wires. We also worked with steam plant operators to make sure that the computer screens were easy to read and helped keep the plant safe."

—John Grube, electrical engineer, Midwest Engineering Group at Duke Energy

PAPER CLIP HELICOPTER

Helicopters are able to fly because of the quickly moving propeller, which provides lift, the force that moves things upward. In this project, you will create your own helicopter. Although this helicopter doesn't have a rotor to make it spin fast enough to fly upward, you will have a chance to learn what causes the blades to spin.

TIME: 15 MINUTES

DIFFICULTY LEVEL: MEDIUM

MATERIALS NEEDED:

- Ruler
- Pencil
- Construction paper
- Scissors
- Paper clip
- Markers (optional)

THE STEPS:

1. Use your ruler to draw a rectangle on your paper that is 2 inches wide and 8 inches long.
2. Cut out the rectangle.
3. Measure 3 inches from the end of your rectangle. Fold the paper and unfold it again.
4. Use the ruler to draw a straight line down the middle from your fold line to the short end of your rectangle. Then cut along the line.
5. Now measure 3 inches from the opposite end of the rectangle and draw a line across the rectangle's width.
6. Use scissors to make a ¼-inch-long cut on both sides of this line.
7. Fold the paper under each of these cuts inward.

8. Then fold the bottom ½ inch of this section up and secure it with a paper clip.

9. Holding your helicopter with the paper clip portion down, fold one of the strips at the top toward you and the other strip away from you. Crease these folds.
10. If you want to decorate your helicopter, now is the perfect time. Use markers to carefully color the 2 folded strips.
11. To fly your helicopter, hold it above your head, with the paper clip portion downward, and let it go.
12. The paper helicopter should twirl as it gently makes its way to the ground.

STEAM CONNECTION: You are using all the components of STEAM in this mechanical engineering challenge. The paper helicopter deals with the science of forces (gravity and air resistance). You are using technology (scissors) as you engineer your helicopter. Art is incorporated if you decorate the blades. And as you measure the paper, you are using math.

Hows & Whys: There are several forces at work here. The first is gravity, which causes the paper helicopter to fall. As it falls, it meets air resistance. The air pushes against both blades with an equal amount of force. Since the blades face in opposite directions, they spin, producing just enough lift to slow the fall.

EXTENSIONS:

- Watch which way your helicopter spins. Then bend the paper blades in the opposite directions. Now what happens?
- Experiment with the size of your blades. What happens if you make the blades longer? What if they are wider?

RUBBER BAND RACE CAR

Have you ever played with one of those toy cars that you roll backward and then it zooms forward on its own? You can engineer your own version of that in this project and explore physics in the process.

TIME: 30 MINUTES

DIFFICULTY LEVEL: CHALLENGING

MATERIALS NEEDED:

- Ruler
- Pencil
- Empty paper towel tube
- Hole punch
- 2 (6-inch) dowel rods
- Colorful duct tape (optional)
- Markers (optional)
- Stickers (optional)
- 4 unwanted CDs
- Masking tape
- Variety of rubber bands
- Paper clip

THE STEPS:

1. Use your ruler and pencil to draw a straight line from one end of the paper towel tube to the opposite end.
2. Slide your hole punch through one end of the paper towel tube as far as it will go and punch a hole along the line you drew. Do the same on the other end.
3. Use your ruler and pencil to draw another straight line on the opposite side of your tube and once again use the hole punch to punch holes at each end of the tube.
4. Slide your dowel rods through the holes. These will be your car's axles. Make sure they are parallel with one another. (You don't want one axle sticking up while the other is resting on the floor.) If necessary, rotate the tube and try again.
5. If you want to decorate your car, this is the perfect time. Take out the dowels, and use colorful duct tape, markers, or stickers to give your car some pizzazz.

6. Insert your dowel rods back through the holes. To keep your CD wheels from slipping off, wrap masking tape around both ends of the dowel rods about one inch from the ends. You will need 2–3 feet of tape for each one, depending on how tightly and smoothly you wrap it.
7. When you are finished, you should be able to push a CD over the taped dowel rod. It should be snug. If it is wobbly, remove the CD and wrap a bit more tape around the dowel rod and try again. Repeat this for the other 3 dowels and CDs.
8. To make your rubber band engine, make a chain with 5 rubber bands. Try to use rubber bands that are the same size. (Thinner rubber bands, around 2 inches long, work best.)
9. Attach your paper clip to the end of the chain.
10. Carefully wrap the paper clip end of your rubber band chain around the back axle of your car, inside the cardboard tube. Then thread the paper clip through the last rubber band of your chain and pull, securing the chain around your axle. You may want to add a piece of tape to help hold the rubber band tight against the axle.
11. Drop the paper clip end through the tube so the rubber band chain is hanging inside the tube. (At this point you may need to remove a rubber band if the chain hangs past the cardboard tube's end.) Secure the paper clip to the cardboard tube, making sure no rubber bands are touching your front axle.

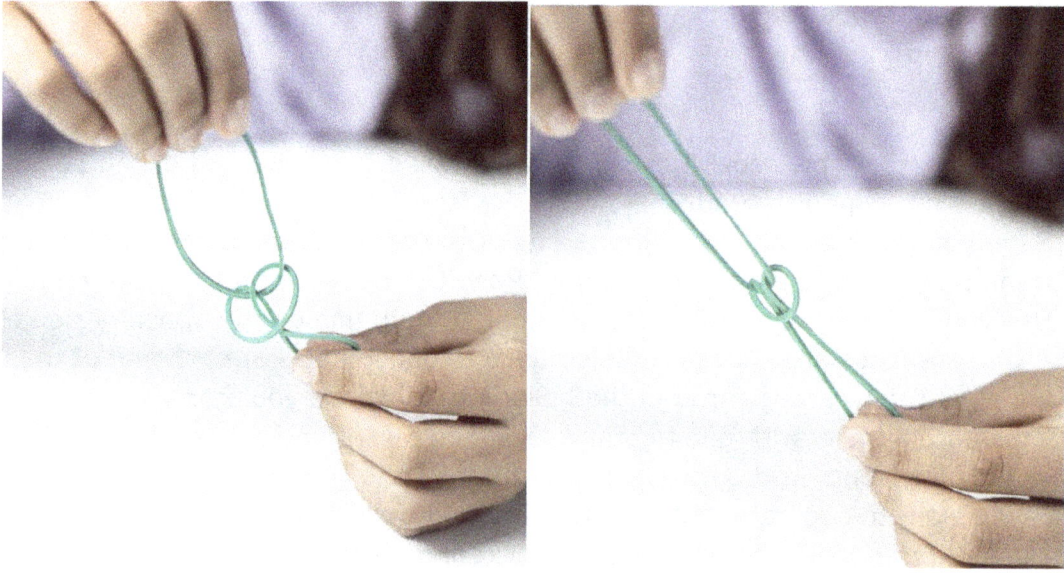

12. To wind your car's engine, hold on to your back axle (the one where the rubber band chain is looped) and rotate the axle to wind the rubber bands around it. (If they don't wind around the axle, try turning it the opposite way.)
13. Keep hold of the axle and set your car on a flat surface. Let go and watch it zoom forward.
14. Remember, part of engineering is trying something and seeing what works and what doesn't. If your wheels are wobbly, the car won't go as far. This project may take some tinkering to make it work properly.
15. If the wheels turn but your car doesn't move, there may not be enough friction between the wheels and the ground. Try the car on a different surface.

STEAM CONNECTION: **In this mechanical engineering project, you used all the components of STEAM. You used science as you dealt with potential and kinetic energy. You used technology when you used the hole punch, ruler, and rubber bands. You used art as you applied masking tape and if you took the time to decorate your race car. You also used math skills to choose the proper length of rubber bands.**

Hows & Whys: As you twist the rubber band around the axle, you are giving it potential energy. The more you twist it, the more potential energy it has. When you let go and the rubber band goes back to its original position, the potential energy is turned into kinetic energy, causing the back axle to spin. When the axle turns, it makes the wheels move, and the car goes forward.

EXTENSIONS:

- What happens if you use thicker rubber bands? Does it affect how far the car travels?
- What happens if you take off a rubber band or if you add one to the chain?
- Try this project with a friend or family member and race your cars. Whose car goes the farthest? Can you figure out why?

MARBLE ROLLER COASTER

Have you ever ridden on a roller coaster? The ride always starts with an exciting drop down a big hill. Lots of smaller hills and sometimes even loops follow. Besides being lots of fun, roller coasters also provide a fun way to explore physics. In this challenge, you will design your very own roller coaster.

TIME: 1 HOUR

DIFFICULTY LEVEL: MEDIUM

MATERIALS NEEDED:

- Scissors
- Pool noodle
- Duct tape
- Table, chair, or kitchen counter
- Paper cup
- Small marbles

CAUTION: Marbles can be a choking hazard for young children. Make sure all marbles are safely put away after this activity.

THE STEPS:

1. Start by cutting the pool noodle in half lengthwise. Now you have 2 pieces of track.
2. Use duct tape to secure one piece of track to the back of a chair, table, or a kitchen counter so that it forms a big hill.
3. Place your paper cup at the bottom of the track.
4. Test out your hill. Place a marble at the top and let it go. The marble should end up in the cup. If it comes off the track, adjust your track.
5. Now comes the fun part! Remove the cup and use your other pool noodle half to continue your track. Use duct tape to attach it to the bottom end of your hill. Make sure when you connect the pieces that you smooth the tape out. A bump in the tape will make your marble jump off the track.
6. You can make a small hill with your new section of track by forming a bump and duct taping it in place to the floor. (Remember to keep your tape smooth.) Or you could make a loop with the new piece of track by curving the free end up and over.

Once you form the loop, use a piece of duct tape to secure the inner parts of the loop. Use more duct tape to hold it in place on the floor. (Sometimes it helps to have someone hold the track pieces while you tape.)

7. Place your paper cup at the end of your track. This will catch your marble for you.
8. Test out your track. Place a marble at the top of the big hill and let it go.
9. If your marble comes off the track, try again. If it continues to come off, loosen the tape and try adjusting the track.

STEAM CONNECTION: You are using lots of science (physics) in this mechanical engineering challenge. You are using technology when you use your scissors to cut the pool noodle. As you design your roller coaster, you will also be using your artistic talents.

Hows & Whys: Just like a real roller coaster, your marble has potential energy when it is at the top of the hill. The energy becomes kinetic energy when you release it and it rolls down the hill. As it rolls, it gains speed and momentum. This enables the marble to continue rolling up future hills. If the marble has enough momentum when it gets to a loop, then centripetal force will keep the marble rolling forward through the circular path.

EXTENSIONS:

- Try making your track even longer by adding additional pool noodles. Can you make a curve? Can you get the marble to go through 2 loops?
- Use other materials, like cardboard boxes, to add other elements to your coaster. Can you make a tunnel?
- How does changing the height of your first hill affect the coaster? Try making the hill taller or shorter.

SCISSOR LIFT GRABBER

Have you ever seen how cars are lifted into the air on platforms so that the mechanics can safely get under the car to work? This kind of device uses a scissor lift, named for the way the beams cross, similar to the way scissors work. Scissor lifts can be used to help lift heavy loads. You can explore the same design engineers use in scissor lifts by making a fun grabber with items you have at home.

TIME: 15 MINUTES

DIFFICULTY LEVEL: CHALLENGING

MATERIALS NEEDED:

- Ruler
- 6 jumbo craft sticks
- Pencil
- Corrugated cardboard
- Pushpins
- Clear tape
- Scissors
- Hot glue sticks
- Pom-poms or paper balls

CAUTION: Be careful when using pushpins. They can be quite sharp.

THE STEPS:

1. Use your ruler to find the middle of each of your jumbo craft sticks. Mark this spot with your pencil.
2. Use your pencil to mark ¼ inch from the ends as well.
3. Place each craft stick, one at a time, onto your corrugated cardboard and use a pushpin to poke a hole into their centers and ¼ inch from each end. The cardboard will help protect the surface you are working on and keep you from poking your finger as you insert the pushpins.
4. To prevent the craft sticks from splitting, try twisting the pushpins as you press them through the wood. If the wood splits at the ends, wrap clear pieces of tape around the craft sticks.

5. Now take 2 craft sticks and place them on top of each other to form an X. Push a pushpin through their center holes to secure them in place.
6. Do the same with the other 4, so you have 3 sets of craft sticks.
7. Place the Xs so the top of one X overlaps the bottom of the next. Use pushpins to secure them together.
8. Cut a hot glue stick into ¼-inch pieces. Stick these pieces over the points of each of the pushpins. These will help hold your grabber together and keep you from getting poked.
9. To use the grabber, hold on to one end and move the craft sticks together and apart.
10. Try picking up small pom-poms or paper balls with your grabber.

STEAM CONNECTION: **In this mechanical engineering activity, you are actually creating a form of technology by applying the science of force. You are also using simple technology and math when you measure with your ruler.**

Hows & Whys: Each pushpin serves as a joint connecting 2 craft sticks together. When you apply force and pull the handle pieces apart, all the Xs get shorter and squished. When you push the handles together, the Xs get taller and your grabber extends.

EXTENSIONS:

- Add more craft stick Xs to see how long you can make your grabber.
- How can you make the grabber more effective? Try wrapping rubber bands to the front set of sticks or constructing different arms to add to it.

RUBBER BAND PADDLEBOAT

Long ago, steam-powered paddleboats were a popular way to transport people and materials up and down the rivers. Eventually other forms of transportation took the place of paddleboats. In this challenge, you will make your own miniature paddleboat to explore how they moved through the water.

TIME: 15 MINUTES

DIFFICULTY LEVEL: MEDIUM

MATERIALS NEEDED:

- Plastic bottle with lid
- Duct tape
- 2 wooden skewers
- Ruler
- Scissors
- 2 plastic spoons
- Rubber band
- Bathtub or large plastic container

CAUTION: Even a small amount of water can be a drowning hazard for small children. Make sure to empty the water from the bathtub or container when finished.

CAUTION: Be careful of the pointy end on the wood skewers. They can be very sharp.

THE STEPS:

1. Lay your bottle on its side and duct tape the wood skewers to the bottle so the skewers are on opposite sides of the bottle. There should be 6 inches of skewer sticking past the bottom of the bottle on both sides.
2. Cut off the bowl of the plastic spoons, leaving ½ inch of the spoon's handle attached to the bowl.
3. Use a thin piece of duct tape to attach the spoon pieces together by their remaining handle pieces so that one bowl faces up and the other down. This will be your boat's paddle.

4. Stretch the rubber band over the skewer ends, from one skewer to the other.
5. Slide your paddle into the rubber band.
6. Test the paddle by twisting it backward in the rubber band. The rubber band should wrap around the paddle. When you release it, the paddle should spin. Make any necessary changes to your boat.
7. Once the paddle is working properly, fill the bathtub with 4–5 inches of water. Twist up the paddle and set your boat in the water to see what happens.

STEAM CONNECTION: Science plays a big role in this mechanical engineering project because you are working with energy and Newton's Third Law of Motion (for every action there is an equal and opposite reaction). You are also using technology in the form of the rubber band. Get creative with your boat design and you'll be adding art in as well.

Hows & Whys: In a steam-powered paddleboat, an engine would turn the paddle wheel. In this version, your rubber band is acting like your engine. When you twist the paddle, you give it potential energy. Releasing it changes that energy to kinetic energy. As the rubber band untwists, it turns your boat's paddles. The paddles push against the water and cause the boat to move forward.

EXTENSIONS:

- How does twisting the rubber band tighter affect the boat?
- Try sliding the rubber band and paddle closer to the boat's body. Does it affect how the boat works? What happens if you move it farther away?
- Can you figure out a way to make your paddleboat into a submarine?

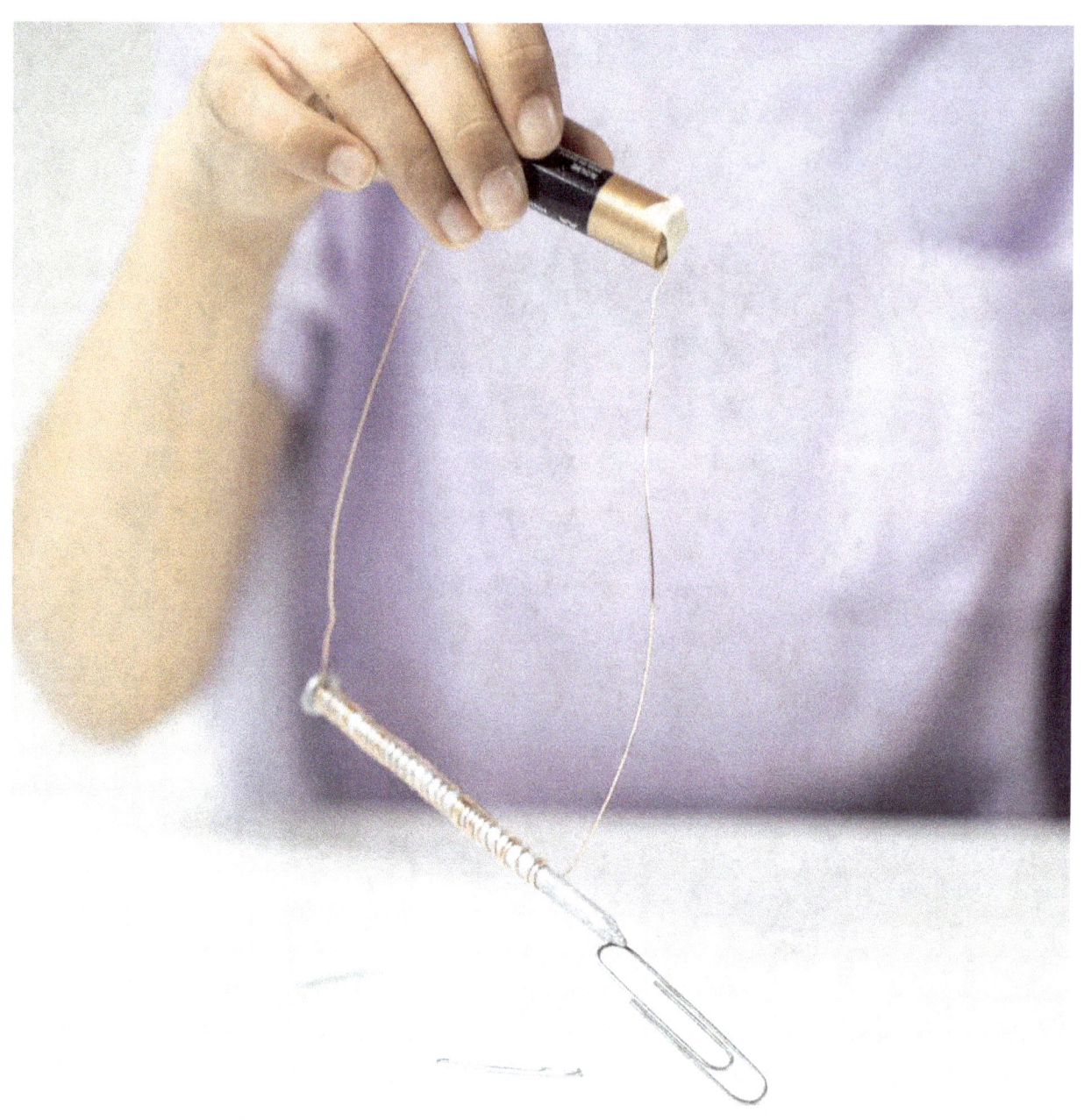

DIY ELECTROMAGNET

Did you know electricity can actually create a magnetic field? Magnets created with electricity are called electromagnets. Electromagnets are used when engineers design and build motors. You can also find electromagnets in MRI machines, music equipment, and even some toys. In this activity, you will build your own electromagnet.

TIME: 20 MINUTES

DIFFICULTY LEVEL: CHALLENGING

MATERIALS NEEDED:

- Scissors
- Thin copper wire
- Large iron nail
- Sandpaper
- Masking tape
- AA cell battery
- Paper clips

CAUTION: Adult supervision is required. The ends of the battery will get very hot during this activity.

THE STEPS:

1. Cut 3 feet of copper wire.
2. Leave 5 inches of wire loose at one end and start wrapping the wire tightly around the nail. Try to wrap the wire as neatly as possible.

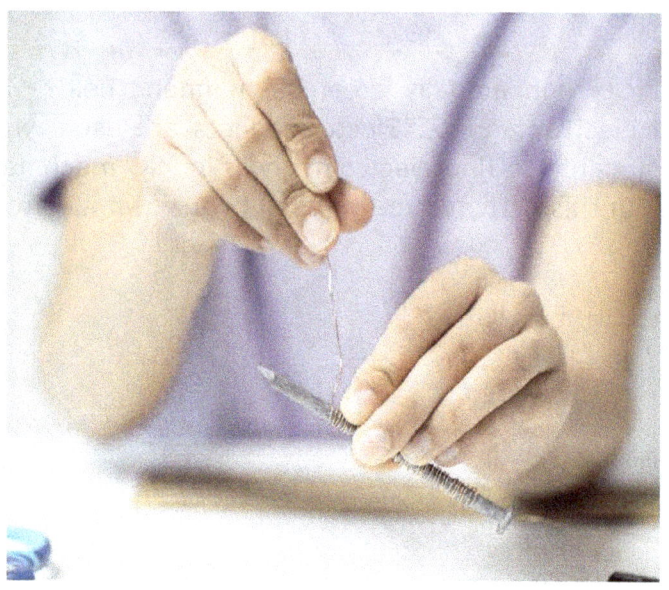

3. Stop wrapping when you have 5 inches of wire left.
4. Use sandpaper to gently remove the outer coating of the last inch of wire on both of your free ends.
5. Tape one end of wire to each end of your battery. You may want an adult to do this step, as the battery will get hot very quickly once both ends of the wire are touching it.

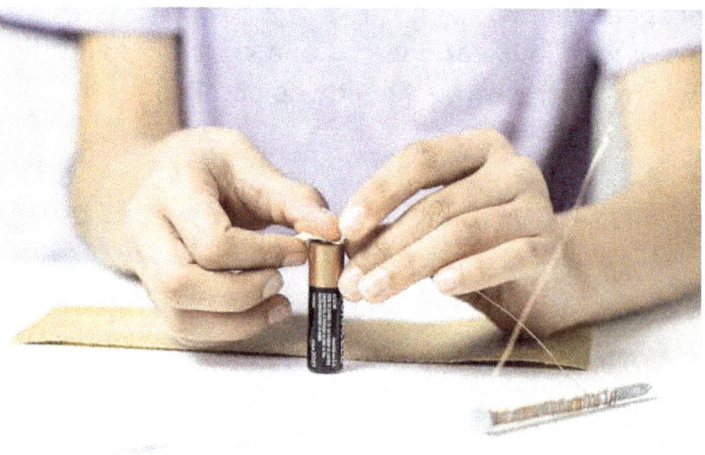

6. Hold the battery by the middle and touch the end of the nail to a paper clip. If your electromagnet has been set up correctly, the nail should now act like a magnet and pick up the paper clip.

Note: The electromagnet will use up the battery quickly, which is why the battery gets hot. Disconnect the wires as soon as you are finished with this activity.

STEAM CONNECTION: This electrical engineering project uses science because it is based on knowledge of physics and electricity. You are using the technology of a battery to create the electromagnet as well.

Hows & Whys: Magnets like those on your refrigerator can't be turned off. An electromagnet like this one is only magnetic when there is electricity. The electricity flows from the battery through the wire and to the nail. It temporarily rearranges the molecules in the nail, making it magnetic.

EXTENSIONS:
- Once you pick up one paper clip, try touching that paper clip to another to form a chain. How many paper clips can you pick up at one time?
- Try using a C or D cell battery. How does this affect your electromagnet?

EGG DROP CHALLENGE

The first automobiles didn't have seat belts, and they certainly didn't have airbags. The safety items that protect us in car crashes today were invented much later. In this challenge, you will engineer a way to protect a raw egg in a crash.

TIME: 45 MINUTES

DIFFICULTY LEVEL: MEDIUM

MATERIALS NEEDED:

- Paper and pencil
- Raw egg
- Tape
- Scissors
- Sturdy chair, step stool, or ladder

OTHER SUGGESTED MATERIALS:

- Small cardboard box or cardboard tubes
- Plastic or paper cups
- Shredded paper, Bubble Wrap, or packing peanuts
- Yarn
- Plastic shopping bags

CAUTION: Adult supervision is required when using a ladder.

THE STEPS:

1. How will you keep your egg from breaking when it's dropped from a 10-foot height? Look over your materials. Sketch out your plan on paper. If you have enough supplies, sketch out a few ideas.
2. Once you have your plan, use your materials to build your solution. Don't forget to include your egg if you are building around it.
3. Take your egg container outside, where it's okay to make a mess.
4. Stand on a sturdy chair, step stool, or ladder and hold your egg container 10 feet from the ground.
5. Drop the container. Then check on your egg. Did it survive the fall without breaking?

STEAM CONNECTION: This mechanical engineering challenge uses science because you are dealing with physics and gravity. Sketching out your design and using creative thinking to come up with your solution involves art. As you measure materials and the height of the egg's drop, you are using math.

Hows & Whys: Gravity causes the egg to fall toward the ground when you let go of the egg container. In order to be successful, you need to figure out how to slow down the speed of the egg. This might be achieved by creating a parachute for the container or adding wings to increase its air resistance (also called drag). You also need to find a way to cushion the impact of the egg hitting the ground.

EXTENSIONS:

- Will your container protect your egg from a higher drop? What if you toss it high in the air and let it fall to the ground?
- Can you design a container that protects an egg using only 2 materials?

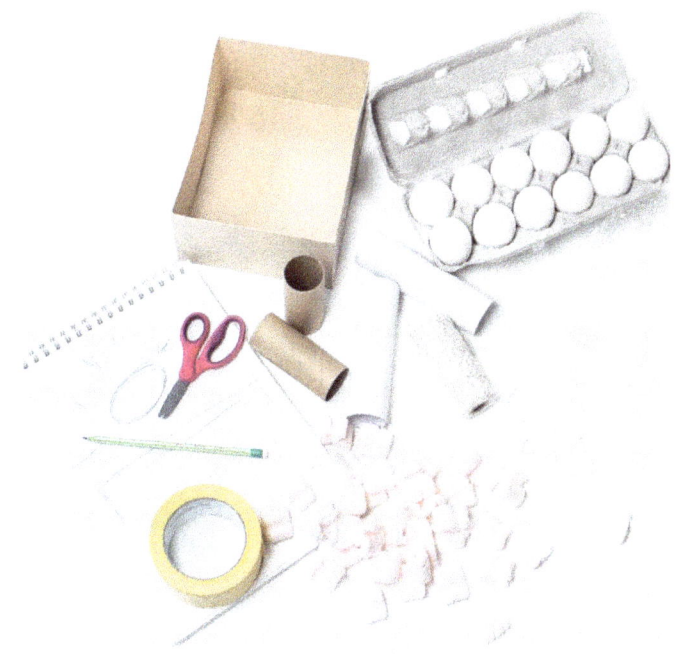

CARDBOARD TUBE MARBLE RUN

Have you ever seen a marble run? You can find them in a variety of types, with brightly colored plastic tubes and funnels. You can learn a lot about physics by making your own marble run with supplies you probably already have at home.

TIME: 30 MINUTES

DIFFICULTY LEVEL: EASY

MATERIALS NEEDED:

- Duct tape
- Paper cup
- Large piece of cardboard or foam board
- Scissors
- Cardboard tubes
- Marbles

CAUTION: Marbles can be a choking hazard for young children. Make sure all marbles are safely put away after this activity.

THE STEPS:

1. Use tape to secure your paper cup in one corner at the bottom of your large piece of cardboard.
2. Choose the opposite corner at the top of your cardboard to be the beginning of the marble run. Your goal is to use the cardboard tubes to get the marble from the starting position into the paper cup.
3. You may cut the tubes however you think will work best. Use small amounts of tape as you position them on the board. Once you are satisfied with their positions, you can use more tape to better secure them.
4. Test how your marble runs through the tubes as you add new tubes. Are marbles flying off the end of the tubes? Try positioning the tubes differently. If marbles are getting stuck, how might you need to tilt the tubes?

STEAM CONNECTION: **Science (physics) plays a big role in this mechanical engineering activity. Gravity causes the marble to travel down the tubes toward**

the cup. You are using technology as you use scissors and tape to build the marble run.

Hows & Whys: At the top of the marble run, the marble has potential energy. This changes to kinetic energy with the help of gravity, as the marble makes its descent. You can increase the speed of the marble by making the cardboard tube steeper.

EXTENSIONS:

- Use a stopwatch and time how long it takes for your marble to reach the cup. Can you design an even faster marble run?

- Cut all your tubes in half lengthwise so they are all open at the top. This will increase the difficulty level.

Notes from the Field

"I entered into this field because computer technology enables everything we do today. The technology is always changing, and there is always something new to learn. My current job is to design and create large-scale automated computer systems that are then used for a wide variety of things, from storing music and pictures to massive data collection and analysis."

—Jerry Schul, computer engineer

CRAFT STICK TRUSS BRIDGE

There are many types of bridges. You may have noticed different types when riding in the car. A truss bridge consists of sides made up of a series of triangles. It is one of the oldest forms of modern bridges. It's also very strong. In this project, you will discover what makes a truss bridge so strong.

TIME: 45 MINUTES

DIFFICULTY LEVEL: CHALLENGING

MATERIALS NEEDED:

- Craft sticks
- Hot glue gun
- Scissors

CAUTION: Hot glue guns get very hot. A parent should assist you when using a hot glue gun.

THE STEPS:

1. Arrange 3 craft sticks into a triangle so their ends overlap. Hot glue them together.
2. Make 5 more triangles, just like the first one, so you have 6 triangles total.
3. Next, lay 3 craft sticks end to end in a straight line.
4. Cut or break another craft stick in half. Hot glue half the craft stick on top of the first craft stick in your line of 3 craft sticks, so it is flush against the far end. Hot glue 2 whole craft sticks on top of the row, so they cover up the seams. Glue the other half from the broken craft stick to the end.
5. Repeat steps 3 and 4 so you have 2 rows of craft sticks.
6. Hot glue the bottoms of 3 of your triangles to one of the rows. Hot glue the other 3 triangles to the other row of craft sticks. These will become the sides of your bridge.
7. Now lay 2 craft sticks end to end in a straight line.
8. Cut or break another stick in half. Hot glue half the craft stick on top of the 2 craft sticks so it is on the very end. Hot glue a full craft stick to cover up the seam between the craft sticks. Then glue the other broken half to the end.
9. Repeat steps 7 and 8 so you have 2 short rows of craft sticks.

10. Hot glue these short rows to the tops of your triangles. Now the bridge's sides are complete.

11. Stand your sides up and hot glue one craft stick flat across from the middle of one side to the other. Hot glue 2 more craft sticks across the bottom, one on each end of your bridge.
12. Hot glue a few more craft sticks across at the bottom, one in the middle of each triangle, and one at the corner of each triangle. These will be supports for the bridge deck.
13. To make the bridge deck, hot glue craft sticks across the supports. Glue the sticks so they touch side to side.
14. For added strength, hot glue one stick across the top of your bridge in the middle and one on each end.

STEAM CONNECTION: **In this civil engineering project, you are using the technology of the hot glue gun. You are also using art and math (geometry) as you build your bridge.**

Hows & Whys: A truss is a structure that consists of a series of triangles. Triangles are a very strong shape. That is because any force added to a triangle is spread out evenly on all 3 sides.

EXTENSIONS:

- How strong is your bridge? Place your bridge so its ends rest on 2 chair seats. Tie a small bucket to hang from the bridge's middle and fill the bucket with weights, sand, or heavy books.
- Try making a longer bridge and testing its strength.

SHAKER INSTRUMENT

Did you know that engineers are needed in the world of music? As music changes to include more and more instruments that are digitally compatible (can be recorded on a computer), engineers are needed to help modify and improve old instrument designs. This includes percussion instruments like drums, cymbals, and shakers, the oldest types of instruments in the world. In this activity, you will engineer and explore the sounds you can create with your very own shaker.

TIME: 10 MINUTES

DIFFICULTY LEVEL: EASY

MATERIALS NEEDED:

- 2 plastic eggs
- Uncooked rice, dried and uncooked beans, or small plastic beads
- Colored tape

THE STEPS:

1. Open one of your plastic eggs and fill one half of it with uncooked rice, uncooked beans, or plastic beads.
2. Close the egg. Make sure it is completely closed. Use colored tape to help keep the egg closed.
3. Fill a second egg with a different filler and seal it shut.
4. Try shaking each shaker, one at a time. What happens? How are they different?

STEAM CONNECTION: You are using science in this engineering activity because you are dealing with sound waves. You are also using art because you are creating a musical instrument, and music is a form of art.

Hows & Whys: When you shake your instrument, the items inside collide with one another and the surface of your container. Sound is created when the objects inside hit the outer shell of the shaker and cause it to vibrate. The vibrations travel through the air in the form of sound waves.

EXTENSIONS:

- Try filling an egg with sand or dirt. Make sure you use tape to seal any small holes in the egg first! How does this filler sound compared with the harder objects?
- How can you make the sound louder? Try using a cardboard tube, empty can, or plastic jar as the body for your shaker.

PIPE CLEANER MAZE

When new stores or houses are planned in an area where there aren't any roads yet, civil engineers have to design roads that will connect these new places to roads that already exist. It's almost like designing a maze. In this activity, you will think creatively as you engineer your own maze.

TIME: 15 MINUTES

DIFFICULTY LEVEL: EASY

MATERIALS NEEDED:

- Shoebox lid or shallow box
- Marker
- Pipe cleaners
- Clear tape
- Marble

CAUTION: Marbles can be a choking hazard for young children. Make sure all marbles are safely put away after this activity.

THE STEPS:

1. Choose a corner of your box. Use your marker to label it with the word *start*. Choose a corner on the opposite side of the box. Use your marker to label it with the word *end*, or draw a star to signify the finish.
2. Your goal is to create a maze that will guide your marble from your starting position to the end.
3. You can cut or bend your pipe cleaners to create your maze. Make it as simple or as tricky as you like. Use tape to hold your pipe cleaners in place. Be careful not to squish your pipe cleaners flat when applying your tape.
4. When you are finished creating your maze, put your marble at *start* and try it out. Hold your box and gently tilt it back and forth to guide your marble through the maze.

STEAM CONNECTION: **When civil engineers design roads, they use all the elements of STEAM to help them. This marble maze is almost like making a road** in that you are creating a path for your marble to travel. You are using science as you deal with the physics of rolling your marble through the maze. You are using technology with your scissors and tape, and designing the maze uses art.

Hows & Whys: As you tilt the box back and forth, the force of gravity will help move the marble. If you go slowly, the marble will stay in the path you created with the pipe cleaners.

EXTENSIONS:

- Get together with a friend and make each other a marble maze to solve.
- Can you figure out a way to make a tunnel on your maze for your marble to go through?

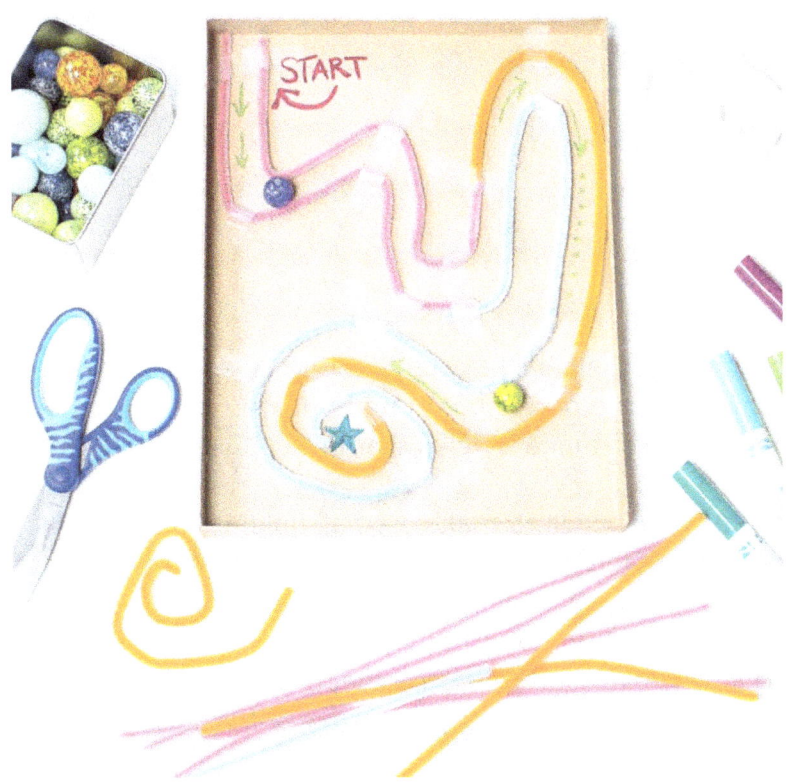

PENDULUM ART

If you've ever used a swing at the playground, you have an idea of what a pendulum is: a weight that is attached to a string or chain and hangs from a fixed point. In this activity, you will build a pendulum and use it to paint.

TIME: 20 MINUTES

DIFFICULTY LEVEL: EASY

MATERIALS NEEDED:

- 2 chairs of equal size
- Broom handle or pole
- Poster board
- Hole punch
- 2 paper cups
- Sharpened pencil
- Yarn
- Tape
- Acrylic paint
- Water

CAUTION: This activity can be messy. It is best to do it outside.

THE STEPS:

1. Place your chairs so their backs face each other and balance your broom handle across them. Place the poster board underneath.
2. Use your hole punch to make 2 holes that are opposite each other in the top of one of your cups.
3. Use the point of your pencil to make a small hole at the bottom of the cup.
4. Thread yarn through the holes at the top of the cup and tie your cup to your broom handle so your cup is about 6 inches from the ground.
5. Put a piece of tape on the bottom of your cup to cover up the hole for now.
6. Squirt some acrylic paint into the other paper cup. Add about twice the amount of water as you did paint. Use your pencil to mix it. You want the paint to be runny.
7. Pour the paint into the hanging cup.

8. Take the tape off the bottom of the cup and hold the yarn to swing the cup into a circular motion.

9. Let go of the yarn and watch your pendulum at work.
10. The paint should drip out of the cup and form a colorful swirl on the poster board, marking the path of the pendulum. If the paint is too thick, it will look like splotches instead of the swirl.

STEAM CONNECTION: In this mechanical engineering activity, you are using science (physics) as you deal with the forces of gravity and friction with your pendulum. You are using technology to punch the holes with your hole punch. And you are creating some colorful artwork as the pendulum swings.

Hows & Whys: Your cup of paint is acting as the weight of your pendulum. When it is hanging and not moving, it is in its equilibrium position. When you move it out of equilibrium, it swings back and forth due to the force of gravity. Friction steals a bit of energy from the pendulum with each swing until it eventually stops. All of this, along with the dripping paint, creates your colorful designs.

EXTENSIONS:

- What happens if you change the length of the string?
- Try swinging your pendulum faster or slower. How does the speed affect your pendulum?

PAPER BRIDGE PENNY HOLDER

Bridges must be strong enough to not only support their own weight, but also the weight of the people and vehicles that go across them. Engineers must consider not only the materials used to build a bridge but also the shape. In this activity, you will discover just how important shape is when it comes to the strength of a structure.

TIME: 15 MINUTES

DIFFICULTY LEVEL: EASY

MATERIALS NEEDED:

- 100 pennies
- Zip-top plastic bag
- 4–6 books
- Ruler
- Construction paper
- Tape

THE STEPS:

1. Put your pennies in a zip-top plastic bag and seal it shut.
2. Stack your books so you have 2 piles that are the same height. Place them so they are 6 inches apart.
3. Take a sheet of paper and lay it across the books like a bridge. Place your bag of pennies on it. What happens?
4. Your goal is to make a bridge out of a sheet of paper. The bridge has to hold the weight of 100 pennies. How can you fold or roll your paper to make it work? You can use tape to hold your paper's shape, but you can't tape it to your books.
5. Before you read any further, take some time to try a few ideas of your own.
6. Now that you've tried a few of your own ideas, try rolling a piece of paper starting at one of the longest sides. You can use a piece of tape to hold the paper in its tube shape. Place it across the space between the books and place the bag of pennies on it so that half the pennies hang on each side of your paper bridge.
7. Now try folding the paper in half so its longest sides touch each other. Then fold the paper into a W shape, so when you look at the shortest side it looks like a W. Will it hold the bag of pennies?

STEAM CONNECTION: In this civil engineering challenge, you are using science as you deal with the gravitational pull of the weight of your pennies. You are also using art as you design your paper bridges and math since you are dealing with weight.

Hows & Whys: The flat piece of paper sagged. Bending or rolling the paper increased its stiffness and allowed you to form a bridge that would hold weight. When you folded the paper in a W shape, you created a series of connected triangles. Triangles form some of the strongest structures. The triangular shapes help make this bridge stronger.

EXTENSIONS:

- Just how much weight will the bridges hold? Try adding more pennies or other coins to your bag to check the strength of the bridge.
- Now move the books farther apart. Can you make a longer bridge that will support the 100 pennies?

MINI NATURE DAM

Beavers are natural engineers. Like beavers, when human engineers design and build dams, they have to create them to be strong enough to withstand the pressure of water flowing. In this challenge, you will discover what it takes to build a dam that works.

TIME: 30 MINUTES

DIFFICULTY LEVEL: MEDIUM

MATERIALS NEEDED:

- Aluminum foil
- Sticks
- Rocks
- Leaves
- Modeling clay
- Access to water and hose or bucket

CAUTION: This activity can be messy. It is best to do it outside.

THE STEPS:

1. Use your aluminum foil to make a small river that is 2–3 feet long. Do this by pulling out 2–3 feet of foil and then fold the sides up 1 inch high. If you want to make your river sturdier, you can double the thickness of the foil.
2. Use your sticks, rocks, and leaves to make a dam in the middle of your foil river.
3. Turn on your hose gently at one end of your river to test your dam. (If you don't have a hose available, you can slowly pour water from a bucket.) Does your dam stay together? Does it keep the water from going past it?
4. Make any adjustments needed to your dam. You can use your modeling clay to help seal any small leaks.
5. Add water to your river and test your dam again. Continue making changes to build the most effective dam you can.

STEAM CONNECTION: **Since you are dealing with forces, you are using science in this civil engineering challenge. You are also using art as you think of a creative way to design your dam.**

Hows & Whys: Water acts like a force against a dam. A dam must be strong enough to support itself and hold back the force of the water. Beavers deal with this force by building their dams in areas where the water flows slowly. Civil engineers deal with the different forces at work by choosing stronger materials, such as concrete, and making sure the dam has a strong foundation to hold it in place.

EXTENSIONS:
- Does the shape of your dam change how effective it is? How does a curved dam compare with one that is straight across?
- Try using wood blocks or dominoes with your modeling clay to create a dam. How effective is it compared with the natural dam you created?

LEMON BATTERY

Look around you. Chances are there is something near you that uses batteries. Batteries help light up flashlights, power watches, and make smartphones work. In this challenge, you will work with electrical engineering and learn how batteries work by making your own with lemons.

TIME: 30 MINUTES

DIFFICULTY LEVEL: CHALLENGING

MATERIALS NEEDED:

- 6 lemons
- 6 shiny pennies
- Soapy water
- Sharp knife
- 6 zinc galvanized nails
- 7 alligator clip battery leads (find at local car parts store or online)
- Mini 5-mm LED bulb

CAUTION: Adult supervision is needed when using sharp knives.

CAUTION: Adult supervision is needed because you are dealing with a low level of electricity.

THE STEPS:

1. Roll and squish your lemons a bit to get their juices flowing. The acid in the juice is necessary to make your battery strong enough to light the LED bulb.
2. Wash your pennies in the soapy water to remove any dirt.
3. Use the knife to make a ½-inch-long slit in each of your lemons. (Depending on the size of your lemons, you might be able to make your battery with just 4. If you want, you can start with 4 and add more if needed.)
4. Slide a penny into the slit of each lemon. You want to make sure your pennies go in far enough to touch the lemon's juicy insides.
5. Next, push a nail into each lemon so only ½ inch of it sticks out. The nail should be about 1 inch away from your penny. You do not want your nail and penny to touch.
6. Arrange your lemons in a circle. This will make it easier to connect them together.

7. Clip one alligator clip to the penny in your first lemon. Fasten the other end of the lead to the nail in the next lemon.
8. Continue connecting your lemons until you get to the last one. On your last lemon connect a clip from one alligator lead to the penny but do not connect it to the next nail. Instead, you will use another alligator clip lead to hook onto the remaining nail. You should then have 2 clips not connected to anything.
9. Attach the 2 remaining clips to the wires on your LED bulb. The clip connected to the penny should clip to the longest wire of the bulb. (This is the bulb's positive side.) Look closely. The bulb should be lit.
10. If your bulb doesn't light up, try unhooking it and turning it to clip it the opposite way. If it still doesn't light up, check all your connections. Make sure the clips are secure and the pennies and nails are far enough into the lemons and do not touch. If it still doesn't work and you opted to try 4 lemons first, try adding another lemon.

STEAM CONNECTION: **You are using science in this electrical engineering challenge as you deal with the chemical reactions taking place. The battery you produce is a form of technology.**

Hows & Whys: In order for a battery to work, you have to have 2 electrodes, separated by an electrolyte. In your battery, the lemon juice is the electrolyte and the zinc nails and copper pennies are acting as the electrodes. Chemical reactions occur inside the lemon where the electrodes touch the juice. These reactions produce electricity as soon as there is a path made with your leads from one electrode to the other. Each lemon is one cell of your battery, so if you use 4 lemons, you have a 4-cell battery.

EXTENSIONS:
- Will other fruits or vegetables be able to produce electricity? Try it with oranges, apples, or potatoes.
- Try using other metals as your electrodes. Instead of pennies you could try nickels or quarters. You could also use different types of nails instead of the zinc ones.

PULLEY BUCKET LIFT

Pulleys are used to pull and lift heavy loads. You'll find pulleys on lots of things, including flagpoles, window blinds, construction cranes, and elevators. In this project, you will learn how pulleys work by building your own simple pulley system.

TIME: 15 MINUTES

DIFFICULTY LEVEL: EASY

MATERIALS NEEDED:

- Something heavy in a bucket (sand, rocks, or a hand weight work)
- 2 chairs of equal size
- Broom handle
- Cardboard tube
- Rope

THE STEPS:

1. Try lifting the filled bucket with one hand. How hard is it to lift up? Your pulley will make it easier!
2. Place your 2 chairs so their backs face each other with your bucket on the ground between them.
3. Balance the broom handle across the chairs.
4. Slide your cardboard tube onto the broom handle so it is in the middle of the chairs. A stronger cardboard tube, like one from aluminum foil, works best, but the tube from a roll of toilet paper will work as well.
5. Tie one end of your rope around the bucket's handle and place your bucket directly under your cardboard tube. Thread the other end up and over your cardboard tube.
6. Try lifting your bucket by pulling on the free end of the rope.

STEAM CONNECTION: In this mechanical engineering project, you are using science (physics) as you deal with the force and energy needed to lift the bucket. The pulley itself is a form of technology.

Hows & Whys: Pulleys usually consist of one or more wheels over which you loop a rope. In your pulley, the cardboard tube is acting as your wheel. With a simple pulley like the one you made in this activity, you are reversing the direction of the force needed to lift the object. It is much easier to use your body and pull down on the rope than it is to use your arm to lift the bucket straight up.

EXTENSIONS:

- Try moving the bucket so it is no longer directly under your pulley system. What happens when you try to lift the bucket?
- Can you figure out how to make a double pulley with another broom handle, cardboard tube, and chairs? (Hint: The rope will go over the first tube and then under the second so you pull up on it.) Which makes it easier to lift the bucket, the single or double pulley system?

TOY ZIP LINE

Have you ever watched a cartoon or movie where one of the characters slides down a long rope or cable? Did you wonder how they did that? Chances are they used a zip line. In this activity, you'll make your own zip line for a toy and get a firsthand look at how they work.

TIME: 20 MINUTES

DIFFICULTY LEVEL: EASY

MATERIALS NEEDED:

- Table, chair, or refrigerator
- Tape measure
- Scissors
- Yarn
- Ruler
- Plastic drinking straw (you can also use a cardboard tube)
- Tape
- Small box
- Pipe cleaners
- Small toy or stuffed animal
- Coins

THE STEPS:

1. Choose a location for your zip line to start. A table, the back of a chair, or even the top of the refrigerator will work. Then choose a place for the zip line to end that is lower to the ground, perhaps the bottom of a kitchen chair or even just a spot on the floor.
2. Use your tape measure to find the distance from where your zip line will start and where it will end.
3. Cut your yarn so it is 6 inches longer than the distance you measured. This will allow for tying or taping it in place.
4. Tie or tape one end of your yarn to your starting point.
5. Cut a 2-inch piece of straw and thread the other end of your yarn through it.
6. Tie or tape the free end of your yarn to your ending spot. Make sure the line is tight.

7. Make sure your box has one side that is open for your toy to sit inside.
8. Use pipe cleaners and tape to attach the box, open-side up, to the straw.
9. Place your toy inside the box and run your zip line to your starting point. Then let it go and see what happens.
10. Add a few coins to the box and send it back down. How does the extra weight affect your zip line?

STEAM CONNECTION: **This challenge uses science (physics) as you deal with gravity, mass, and friction. You are using scissors and tape, forms of technology, to create the zip line. The zip line itself is also a form of technology. You are using math when you measure the yarn. When designing a real zip line, engineers would also use math to make calculations regarding the weight of the zip line and how much weight it can hold and still move.**

Hows & Whys: A zip line is basically a cable that starts higher than where it ends. It uses the downward slope of the cable, along with gravity, to work. You also need to reduce the friction on the cable. Most zip lines use a wheel for this. You used a straw or cardboard tube to help reduce the friction on your zip line.

EXTENSIONS:
- Add a few more coins to your zip line box. What happens?
- Increase the slope of your zip line (make it steeper). How does that affect the speed of the zip line box?

SCRIBBLE BOT

Do you like drawing? What if you could create your very own robot that produces art? In this activity, you will build a device that will draw for you. Although it won't be a true robot since it isn't programmed by a computer, this activity will introduce you to the world of robotics.

TIME: 20 MINUTES

DIFFICULTY LEVEL: MEDIUM

MATERIALS NEEDED:

- Scissors
- Pool noodle
- Rubber band
- Markers
- Ruler
- Large piece of art paper
- Electric toothbrush (an inexpensive, skinny, lightweight one works best)

THE STEPS:

1. Cut a 6-inch piece from your pool noodle.
2. Use your rubber band to attach 3 markers to the pool noodle so the tips of the markers hang 1 inch off the edge of the pool noodle. The markers should be evenly spaced around the noodle. Make sure it stands up on the markers. Arrange them as needed.
3. Place your scribble bot on your large piece of paper so it sits on the marker tips.
4. Turn on the electric toothbrush and slide it into the hole of the pool noodle, bristle-side down, so the top of the toothbrush touches the paper.
5. The scribble bot should move across the paper, decorating it as it goes.

STEAM CONNECTION: In this electrical engineering activity, you are using the technology of an electric toothbrush to power your scribble bot. You are also engaging in creating art as your scribble bot produces your very own colorful artwork.

Hows & Whys: There are many different ways you can make a scribble bot, but they all deal with an unbalanced motor that makes it move in funny ways. As the motor in the toothbrush vibrates it causes the scribble bot to move, leaving the design drawn by the markers.

EXTENSIONS:

- What happens when you raise or lower the markers on the pool noodle?
- Can you get your scribble bot to work with other drawing items? Try crayons, colored chalk, or paintbrushes and paint instead of markers.

NEEDLE-AND-CORK COMPASS

Long ago, sailors used the stars to help guide them as they traveled. Magnetic compasses were an important invention because they allowed sailors to determine the direction even if clouds hid the stars. In this activity, you will engineer your own compass and explore how it works.

TIME: 15 MINUTES

DIFFICULTY LEVEL: MEDIUM

MATERIALS NEEDED:

- Shallow bowl
- Water
- Scissors
- Cork
- Magnet
- Metal sewing needle
- Tape
- Compass (one on a smartphone is fine)
- Permanent marker

CAUTION: Be careful when handling sewing needles; they are very sharp.

CAUTION: Magnets can be dangerous to small children. Keep magnets away younger kids and from electronic devices like computers and smartphones.

THE STEPS:

1. Fill your shallow bowl halfway with water.
2. Cut off a ¼-inch piece of cork, so you have a small cork disk.
3. Rub your magnet against the sewing needle from top to bottom at least 30 times. Make sure you always run it in the same direction. Put your magnet somewhere safe, away from the compass you are building.

4. Use a small piece of tape to fasten the needle to the top half of your cork disk. Place it on top of the water, in the middle of the bowl.
5. When the cork disk and needle stop moving, use your compass to determine where north is. Use your permanent marker to mark the end of the needle pointing north.
6. You now have a working compass!

STEAM CONNECTION: **Since you are dealing with the effects of magnets and friction, you are using science in this engineering activity. The compass you create is a form of technology.**

Hows & Whys: Rubbing the magnet against the needle turns it into a weak, temporary magnet. Because magnets interact with one another, your magnetized needle interacts with Earth's magnetic field. For the compass to work, you also need to remove as much friction as possible. Floating the needle on water does this.

EXTENSIONS:

- Move a magnet near your compass. What happens?
- If you have magnets of different strengths, try making a few compasses with other needles. How do the compasses compare?

POM-POM POPPER

Have you ever used a confetti popper? When you pull the string, confetti flies out. It's fun to use at parties. In this activity, you will make your own popper that shoots confetti or pom-poms. It's a fun way to learn about energy and motion.

TIME: 10 MINUTES

DIFFICULTY LEVEL: EASY

MATERIALS NEEDED:
- Balloon
- Scissors
- Cardboard tube
- Colored duct tape
- Pom-poms

CAUTION: Balloons can be choking hazards for small children. Make sure to dispose of used balloons properly when finished.

THE STEPS:
1. Tie a knot in the end of your balloon.
2. Snip off the top end of your balloon.
3. Stretch the balloon over one end of your cardboard tube and secure it with duct tape.
4. If desired, you can decorate the remaining portion of your cardboard tube with duct tape as well.
5. Put a few pom-poms in your popper and let them fall into the balloon.
6. Hold the popper in one hand. Pull back on the balloon with your other hand and then let go.
7. The pom-poms should fly out.

STEAM CONNECTION: In this mechanical engineering activity, you are using science with Newton's First Law of Motion as well as potential and kinetic energy. You also used the technology of scissors and tape to build the pom-pom shooter. You used art if you decorated your tube.

Hows & Whys: This activity is an example of Newton's First Law of Motion (sometimes referred to as the law of inertia), which says an object at rest stays at rest unless acted on by an unbalanced force. In this case, the pom-poms would stay at rest, but they are acted upon with the force of the balloon when you pull it back and let go. The balloon is also an example of potential energy changing to kinetic energy.

EXTENSIONS:

- How does the way you pull back on the balloon affect the way your pom-pom travels? Try pulling it back as far as you can versus pulling it back just a little. Now try pulling the balloon back at an angle.
- Does the size of the pom-pom used make a difference in how far it travels? Try using a small pom-pom a few times and then a larger pom-pom.

CLOTHESPIN BALANCING STICK

Have you ever wondered how someone can walk on a tightrope without falling? They have to keep their center of gravity directly over the tightrope in order to keep their balance. Engineers also deal with the center of gravity when designing and building structures like skyscrapers. You can learn about the center of gravity and amaze your friends and family with this simple activity.

TIME: 10 MINUTES

DIFFICULTY LEVEL: MEDIUM

MATERIALS NEEDED:

- Craft stick
- Pipe cleaner
- 2 clothespins

THE STEPS:

1. First, try balancing the craft stick on its end. Right now it won't work, but it will in just a bit.
2. Bend your pipe cleaner in half to find its center and then open it back up.
3. Wrap the center of the pipe cleaner around your craft stick, about 1 inch from the end of the craft stick. Then wrap it back around to the other side of the craft stick.
4. Make sure there is an equal amount of pipe cleaner hanging on both sides of the craft stick. If it isn't equal, you can try wrapping it again or use scissors to trim it so it is even.
5. Clip a clothespin to each end of pipe cleaner.
6. Place the end of the craft stick that is closest to where the pipe cleaner is wrapped on your fingertip or someone else's fingertip.
7. Move the pipe cleaner slightly if needed to get the craft stick to balance on its end.

STEAM CONNECTION: **In this mechanical engineering challenge, you are using science as you deal with the center of gravity. You are also using technology when you use the clothespins, which are actually a type of lever that has been modified to help hang up clothes.**

Hows & Whys: You can balance the craft stick on its end because you changed the craft stick's center of gravity. Originally it is in the middle of the craft stick. When you add the pipe cleaner and clothespins toward the bottom and let them hang down, the center of gravity is lowered, making it easier to balance the stick on its end.

EXTENSIONS:

- Can you get it to balance on your finger with the craft stick turned sideways?
- Try replacing the materials you used with other items. Replace the craft stick with a pencil, or use metal washers instead of clothespins.

GRAPHITE CIRCUIT DRAWING

What do you need in order to light up a light bulb? In this fun activity, you will actually create a piece of art that lights up. At the end of the project, you will have a basic understanding of how electrical circuits work.

TIME: 15 MINUTES

DIFFICULTY LEVEL: MEDIUM

MATERIALS NEEDED:

- Graphite art pencil (find in an art supply store or online)
- White paper
- Clear tape
- Mini 5-mm LED bulb
- 9-volt battery

CAUTION: Adult supervision is required when working with electricity.

THE STEPS:

1. Use your graphite pencil to draw half a circle about 3 inches wide on your paper. You want your line to be ¼-inch thick.
2. Draw the other half of the circle, leaving a ¼-inch space between the top and the bottom of the circle halves.

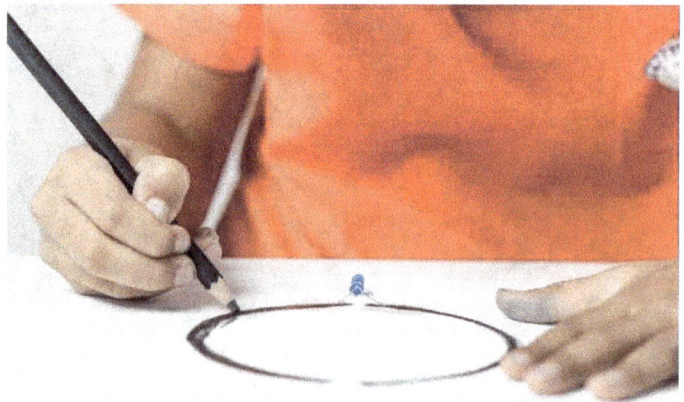

3. Use 2 small pieces of tape to fasten your LED bulb wires at the bottom of your circle so one wire touches one half of the circle and the other wire touches the other half.
4. Place your 9-volt battery upside down on the top of your circle so the positive prong is on the line of one half of the circle and the negative prong is on the line of the other half of the circle.
5. The light bulb should light up. If it doesn't, turn your battery around so the prongs touch the opposite sides of the circle.

STEAM CONNECTION: **You are using science in this electrical engineering activity. You are also using the technology of a battery and light bulb. Since drawing is involved, you are also incorporating art in this activity.**

Hows & Whys: Graphite is a conductor, meaning electricity can travel along its length. When you place the battery on top of the circle and the LED bulb connects the gap at the bottom, you close the circuit. The electricity from the battery is able to travel along the graphite lines to the LED bulb and light it up.

EXTENSIONS:

- Will it work on a larger graphite circuit? Draw a larger shape on your paper, making sure to leave 2 spots open to place the LED bulb and battery.
- Can you get the circuit to work with 2 LED bulbs? Draw another shape, leaving 3 spaces to place your battery and 2 separate LED bulbs.

SIMPLE SHELTER

Imagine you have gotten lost while hiking in the woods. It's getting dark, and it looks like it may rain. You need a shelter until you can be rescued, but you don't have a tent with you. Luckily, you brought a tarp so you'd have something to sit on while you enjoyed your picnic lunch. In this engineering challenge, you will learn how to make a simple shelter out of your tarp.

TIME: 20 MINUTES

DIFFICULTY LEVEL: MEDIUM

MATERIALS NEEDED:

- Rope
- 2 trees near each other, swing set, or clothesline poles
- 1 (6 x 8-foot) tarp
- Medium-size rocks or metal tent stakes

THE STEPS:

1. Tie one end of your rope to a tree. Tie it at the height you want the top of your shelter to be. Three feet off the ground should work well. (If you do not have an area with trees you can use, you can also try using the poles of a swing set, clothesline poles, or something similar.)
2. Stretch your rope to your second tree and tie it at the same height.
3. Lay your tarp over the rope so 4 feet of tarp hangs from each side.
4. Stretch out one side of the tarp so the end just touches the ground and secure it in place. You can do this by placing several rocks along the edge. Or, if you have metal tent stakes, you can push a stake through the grommets (the metal rings) on the ends of the tarp and into the ground.
5. Once one side is secure, stretch out the other side of the tarp and secure it in place like you did the first side.

STEAM CONNECTION: **In this civil engineering challenge, you are using science as you build a shelter to protect you from the rain and wind, two elements that can**

cause you to lose body heat. You are also using a form of technology when you use the tarp, which is made from a waterproof material.

Hows & Whys: When you build your shelter in a triangular form like this one, it allows any possible rain to roll down the sides of the tarp instead of collecting on top where it could get heavy and destroy the shelter. The sides of the tarp will help protect you from wind if you angle the shelter correctly.

EXTENSIONS:

- Use your rope and tarp to build a shelter with only one open side instead of two. You can do this by tying the rope to your second tree so it is lower to the ground. You will also need to secure your tarp to the rope to keep it from sliding.
- How else could you build a shelter? Experiment with your rope and tarp.

Notes from the Field

"My job is to understand my company's goals and design solutions that match those needs. The limitless possibilities of making something work from just an idea is a very fulfilling feeling for me. As the IT industry and my own experience and knowledge grow, I get to see technology shape our culture in numerous and tremendous ways."

—Mark Campbell, computer engineer

Part Three PUTTING IT ALL TOGETHER

You finished the projects. Now what?

Let's take a moment to consider what you've learned. You've learned about the engineering design process and what it takes to be an engineer.

And doing the projects has taught you much more than just engineering skills. By working the activities in part 2, you've also gained skills that will help you throughout life. You've learned how to think creatively and not give up when things don't work out as planned. These skills are important no matter what career you choose.

I'M AN ENGINEER!

As you worked through the projects in this book, you were encouraged to **ask** questions. You've learned to think creatively and **imagine** possible solutions. In several projects, you drew a **plan** to guide you through the design process. You've worked to **create** a variety of projects and then went back to **improve** their designs.

Those are all steps of the engineering design process that engineers use each day (ask, imagine, plan, create, improve). You've become an engineer!

The challenges have taught you a lot more than just how to use the engineering design process. The activities in this book have taught you to problem-solve. The first step is to realize there is a problem. But the world needs people who go much further than that. We need people like you who look for solutions and make the world a better place to live.

And by working on projects like the Paper Tower and Mini Nature Dam, you've learned that there can be more than one solution.

When activities didn't go as planned, you learned to persevere and not give up. Sometimes you were able to make improvements and get the project to work the way you wanted. But even when it didn't work out, you learned an important lesson—it's okay to fail. We learn through our mistakes, and those who keep going after defeat often make the biggest discoveries.

What I really hope you learned through doing the engineering projects in this book is that learning can be fun.

ENGINEERING ALL AROUND YOU

Remember all the hows and whys that were given for each project? They were full of science concepts that were involved in your engineering.

You did several projects that demonstrated potential and kinetic energy. Think about the marble at the top of the Cardboard Tube Marble Run or the rubber band in the Crafty Rubber Band Shooter. You encounter potential and kinetic energy every day. The gasoline sitting in the tank of a car has potential energy. It changes to kinetic energy when the car is started and travels down the road. There is potential energy when you are holding a ball in your hand, and it changes to kinetic energy when you throw the ball and it moves through the air.

Remember the Lemon Battery and Graphite Circuit Drawing? Both of those dealt with electricity moving through a circuit. When you flip a switch to turn on the lights in your house, electricity moves through a circuit—just as it did in those projects. The activities you did allowed you to visualize what you can't always see in the electrical devices that you encounter each day.

You also had the chance to engineer and learn about a few simple machines. Simple machines are used every day to help make tasks easier. In several activities, you encountered levers, which can be used to help lift objects. Have you ever played on a seesaw or used a shovel? Those are both examples of levers you probably have used in real life.

You built a pulley and learned how it can help make it easier to lift heavy objects. Elevators are just one type of pulley you will find in the world around you. You also had the opportunity to explore how axles work. Besides cars and other wheeled vehicles, you will find this simple machine being used in windmills, on shopping carts, and in ceiling fans.

ENGINEERS RULE

As you've been working through the projects in this book, you may have started to notice how engineering affects your life every day.

The button you push to make the car window go up and down—an engineer designed that. Look out of the window as you're riding in a car. A civil engineer helped plan how the roads connect. When you pass over a bridge, check out how it's built. Its design and the materials used were all chosen by engineers.

Do you have a favorite video game? A software engineer (a type of electrical engineer) designed it. And your favorite flavor of that extra chewy bubble gum? That's right, a chemical engineer played a part in making that happen.

What new inventions will happen in your lifetime? What technological advances will we see? What problems would you like to see solved?

Remember, it all starts with asking questions. As an engineer you need to think about how the problem could be solved. What's been tried so far and how can it be improved?

Imagine the possibilities.

You could help design cars that avoid collisions. Or you might create a system that supplies clean drinking water to people all over the world. Maybe you'll develop the hottest video game of the year.

Even if you choose not to go into a career that involves engineering, the skills you've learned through these engineering projects will help you contribute to the world around you.

GLOSSARY

air resistance: the force of friction that air has against a moving object; sometimes referred to as drag

anemometer: wind meter, used to measure wind speed

axle: the rod connected to the center of a circular object, such as a wheel, that allows it to turn

center of gravity: the point where the weight of an object is even on all sides

centripetal force: force that acts on an object moving in a circular path that keeps it moving along that circular path

chemistry: one of the main branches of science that studies the substances that make up matter

circuit: a source of electricity and the complete path that the electricity can flow around

conductor: material that allows electricity to flow through it easily

debug: to remove errors

drag: the force of friction that air has against a moving object; sometimes referred to as air resistance

displacement: to physically move out of position; when a submerged object takes up the space that would normally be taken up by water, the object will float as long as it weighs less than the amount of water it displaces

electrode: an electrical conductor that carries electricity and is used to touch a non-metal part of a circuit

electrolyte: an acid or salt that, when dissolved, can conduct an electric current

electromagnet: a piece of iron that becomes a temporary magnet when an electric current flows through it

energy: the ability to do work; how things change and move

engineering design process: a series of steps engineers use as they work to solve problems—ask, imagine, plan, create, improve; sometimes referred to as EDP

equilibrium: a state of balance between opposing forces

force: a push or pull on an object

friction: a force that slows or stops movement between two objects that are in contact with each other

fulcrum: the place on a lever that allows the lever to move back and forth

geometry: branch of math that deals with points, lines, and shapes

gravity: the force that tries to pull two objects toward each other; Earth's gravity is what causes objects to fall

inertia: simply put, an object stays at rest or continues moving at the same speed unless something forces it to change; Newton's First Law of Motion
insulator: a material that can't carry electricity through it
kinetic energy: energy of motion
lever: a simple machine made of a long body that rests on a support (fulcrum) and can be used to lift things with less effort
lift: the upward force created by the difference in air pressure that keeps airplanes in the air
magnetism: a force that can attract (pull closer) or repel (push away) objects made of a magnetic material
mass: the amount of matter an object is made of
matter: anything that takes up space
molecules: the smallest unit of a substance that has all the properties of the substance
momentum: the strength or force something has when it is moving
pendulum: a weight that hangs from a wire or string that is attached to a fixed point
physics: branch of science that studies matter and energy
polymer: molecules bonded together to form a long chain
potential energy: stored energy an object has because of its position
prototype: an early model of a product made to test how it works
pulley: a simple machine made with wheels and a rope to help move objects
revolutions per minute (RPM): the measure of rotational speed; how many turns occur in one minute
slope: how steep something is
solar: having to do with the sun
speed: how fast an object moves
technology: the use of science to invent tools or solve problems
tension: a force that stretches or pulls on something
thrust: a force that pushes objects forward and increases velocity
truss: a framework made of many triangles
velocity: how fast an object moves in a certain direction
vertex: the point where two or more edges, lines, or curves meet
vibrate: to move rapidly back and forth
weight: the force of gravity on an object

RESOURCES

These websites include tons of fun engineering and STEAM activities.

TheresJustOneMommy.com/stem-activities:
Fun STEM activities for kids 5–12

TeachEngineering.org:
Digital library collection of engineering lesson plans for K–12 educators

ScienceBuddies.org:
Science fair project ideas for kids and STEM lesson plans for teachers

ScienceKids.co.nz:
Engineering and science projects, online games, lesson plans, quick facts, and science quizzes

FrugalFun4Boys.com:
Fun technology and engineering activities for boys and girls

TeachersTryScience.org:
STEM lessons and resources for educators and science activities for kids

www.ingramcontent.com/pod-product-compliance
Lightning Source LLC
Chambersburg PA
CBHW081358070526
44583CB00020B/2589